YOU CAN'T SCARE ME!

A GUIDE TO THE STRANGE AND SUPERNATURAL

Copyright © *ticktock* Entertainment Ltd 2002

This revised edition published in 2009

First published as Ghosts, Monsters and the Unexplained in 2002 by *ticktock* Media Ltd,
The Old Sawmill, 103 Goods Station Road, Tunbridge Wells, Kent, TN1 2DP

ISBN: 978 1 84898 066 2
Printed in China
9 8 7 6 5 4 3 2 1

Picture credits (t=top; b=bottom; c=centre; l=left; r=right; OFC=outside front cover; OBC=outside back cover):
AKG: 9tr, 8-9b, 11b, 14 (main), 15t, 17br, 18t, 34-35b, 34-35c, 35cr, 35tr, 36-37 (main), 37cl, 37tl, 40tl, 41r, 42tr, 42-43c, 43br, 46b, 46c, 48cl,
50c, 57c, 58-59c, 60c, 64tl, 68cb, 70-71b, 72tl, 73br, 79c, 82tl, 123cr. Allsport: 10b. British Museum: 65t. Alastair Carew-Cox; 125cr.
J. Allan Cash: 29r. CFCL: 38l. Colorific: 64-65. Corbis: 6tl, 11 (main), 12-13c, 17tr, 19b, 22 (main), 22br, 23b, 26tl, 30bl, 30-31 (main), 31tr,
39tr, 41cl, 49tr, 58c, 64-65b, 66bl, 74-75b, 76bl, 84cl, 84tl, 84-85c, 104bl, 106b, 118-119 (main). Corbis Royalty Free Images: 108-109.
Et Archive: 52-53t, 70-71t. Fortean Picture Library: 2, 8-9c, 12t, 13r, 15cl, 16br, 19c, 20tl, 20c, 20-21b, 21 (main), 23tr, 24 (main), 24-25t,
25tr, 30tl, 32b, 36tl, 40-41c, 50-51bc, 50tl, 51c, 51, 54c, 54b, 57tr, 57bc, 59c, 55tr, 60b, 62 (main), 62-63c, 63b, 63tr, 66-67c, 68l, 68-69ct,
69bl, 70c, 70-71c, 72-73c, 75tr, 80bl, 80-81b, 84b, 85b, 84-85t, 86tr, 87br, 88b, 88-89c, 89br, 89tr, 90/91cb, 92b, 92c, 93bl, 94-95b, 95tr, 96bl,
97br, 96-97b, 98tl, 99c, 98-99b, 98-99t, 100c, 100tl, 100-101b, 100-101t, 101br, 105tl, 106-107c, 109tr, 109bl, 110tl, 110cl, 111tl, 111cr,
111cl, 112b, 113b, 114tr, 118bl, 121b, 122tl, 124-125t. Gamma: 71t. Geoscience: 74bl. Giraudon; 124tl. Groomwatch; 104t. Image Bank:
16t, 32tl. Images; 24-25c, 33 (main), 117r. Images CWP: 43tr, 52tl, 58-59t, 76bl, 90-91t. Image Select: 6b, 16-17c, 22b, 31br, 60-61b, 63c,
67tr, 72bl, 74-75t, 76c, 83tr, 86b, 123t. iStock: OBC, 107r. Kobal: 96-97t. Mary Evans Picture Library: 50-51c, 90cl, 92-93c, 93cr, 99c,
107bl, 110cr, 110br, 111br, 112bl, 115tr. Pictor: 118c, 119tr. Planet Earth Pictures: 27r, 121tc, 48tl, 48-49br, 52-53c. Plymouth City
Museum & Art Gallery: 19t. Rex Features: 55tl, 56, 56tr, 56-57c, 120bc. Ronald Grant Archive: 18 (main). Ann Ronan @ Image Select:
4b, 8tl, 15bl, 20l, 23cr, 26b, 27b, 27tr, 39c, 44c, 44cr, 45, 50tl, 52bl, 53cr, 61tr, 66tl, 87c, 91b, 125br. Science Photo Library: 3, 4-5tc, 32tr,
82bl, 82-83c, 86tl, 90tl, 94c, 94-95t, 95cr, 102cb, 102-103cb, 102tl, 102ct, 103, 112tl, 114l, 120tl. Spectrum Colour Library: 8bl, 15br, 118tl.
Shutterstock: OFC, 1, 112-113, 29tr. Telegraph Colour Library: 46-47c, 46tl, 48c, 48-49tc, 54tl, 55 (main), 66c, 116-117t, 120cr, 120-121tc.
The Kobal Collection: 27 (main), 34tl, 39tl, 44tl, 44b, 104bl, 106tl, 114c, 114-115. Tony Stone Images: 6-7c, 7 (main), 10tl, 12-13 (main),
25b, 28b, 28t, 28-29 (main), 29br, 64bl, 76-77c, 77tr, 78, 80c, 80tl, 83c, 87 (main), 104-105c, 117cb, 122-123(main).
WENER FOREMAN: 40b, 73tr.

CONTENTS

The unexplainable mysteries in life intrigue a great number of us. Is this because there is something irresistible about the things we have no answer for? Or is it the mere suggestion that there might be life beyond our Earthly sphere that starts our blood racing? Despite the fact that all these paranormal phenomena are unable to be explained by scientists, a lot of evidence has been gathered together to support the claims of those who believe they have witnessed or experienced something otherworldly.

INTRODUCTION

GHOSTS, MONSTERS, & THE SUPERNATURAL

Unidentified Flying Objects; monsters on land and in the sea; ghosts and werewolves; witches and warlocks – do any of these things really exist? What about people who claim they have received a message from beyond the grave? How about those who believe they have had accurate visions of the future? This book takes you past the hype, and shows you real case studies to help you make up your own mind.

SUPERNATURAL IN LITERATURE

Much has been written about the supernatural world. One of the earliest spooky novels was Bram Stoker's Dracula. Ghosts often featured in Shakespeare plays, and novels about beings from other planets are called 'science fiction'. Read about why these subjects have never ceased to delight audiences through the ages.

SCIENCE OF THE PARANORMA / GHOSTBUSTING

The scientific study of unexplainable phenomena is known as 'para-psychology'. 'Paranormal' describes any unusual experience that we don't have an explanation for, based on our understanding of life on Earth. Paranormal experiences generally seem strange, unbelievable, or unnatural to human beings. Find out about the cutting-edge science being used to investigate the unexplained.

FAKES & FRAUDS

For the number of people who have truly observed otherwoldly phenomena, there are just as many stories that turn out to be quite false. You'll be surprised at the lengths some people will go to to make a profit! From dubious photos of UFOs over cityscapes to supposed sea-serpent sightings – make up your own mind about the belieavability of some of the amazing sights many have witnessed.

CULTURES & THE UNEXPLAINED

Many cultures and religions believe in life beyond this world. Find out all about the otherworldly beliefs of cultures such as Buddhists, Shamans and ancient Egyptians. Despite many differences in their beliefs, there is clearly something about the unexplained that fascinates, just as much as it baffles, most of us.

WHAT IS A GHOST?

Nobody really knows what a ghost is. Despite the long history of recorded sightings, no basic facts have ever been agreed. Modern researchers continue to investigate the subject, but until more is known, the question of whether or not ghosts exist remains largely a matter of faith. Perhaps the most persistent belief is that ghosts are spirits of the dead. This inevitably links the subject with the larger issues of religious belief, cultural superstitions and scientific theory. Whatever our views, the numerous accounts of extraordinary ghostly sightings and events makes this fascinating phenomenon hard to ignore. Why are there reports of ghosts right across the globe, and what truth lies behind these strange sightings?

TRICKS & PRANKS

Many photographs of ghosts have proven to be fakes. Ghostly pictures were popular at the end of the 19th century when photography was a new technology. The easiest photographic trick is that of double exposure. This is when two separate shots are taken on the same piece of film, resulting in one image being superimposed over another.

PERCEPTIONS

The image of a ghost that comes to mind for most people is a pathetic figure, clothed in a white gown, rattling chains and perhaps dragging a ball and manacle behind it. In reality, such an obvious manifestation is rare. Most ghosts seem to appear only once, usually at the moment of their death, and never return to haunt their former home. Many people who claim to have seen a ghost report the experience as a positive and uplifting one. They only feel fear as the ghost begins to materialize.

THE AFTERLIFE

Throughout history, most cultures have believed in some form of afterlife. The ancient Egyptians made elaborate preparations for the journey into the afterlife by mummifying and preserving a body after death. The Christian Church promises resurrection of the human soul after death. Ghosts are sometimes thought to be souls or spirits trapped on Earth, unable to pass over to the spiritual plane.

FANTASTIC LIGHTS

Some ghosts may be attributable to natural phenomena. In the past, fantastic lights such as the *aurora borealis* around the North Pole could have been mistaken for spiritual visitations. A common phenomenon known as will-o'-the-wisp has often been mistaken for ghosts. For centuries, these mysterious pale lights have been seen hovering over marshland. Rather than spirits of the dead, they are the spontaneous combustion of marsh gasses.

FOOD FOR THOUGHT

People on the brink of death have experienced seeing a tunnel of ephemeral white light apparently beckoning them into the afterlife. Recent scientific research suggests a physical rather than a spiritual explanation for these near-death experiences. Sensory deprivation is known to produce hallucinations in the brain. Also, lack of oxygen to the brain could stimulate cells in the cortex which would induce the tunnel and white light effect.

WHAT IS A MONSTER?

Why do we feel the need to be afraid? Monsters are borne out of the dark, out of the unknown, out of the things that human beings don't fully understand. Our ancestors' fears were often justified, and deep in all our souls there still lives a cave-dweller, ever-fearful of wild animals, ever-worried about where the next meal will come from, ever-terrified of the dark, of thunder, lightning, loneliness and desertion. Such instinctive fears make us all too willing to believe in monsters. Even today, many people continue to be afraid of the dark because it represents the unknown. With the lights off, our eyes fail us, our other senses can become confused or even desert us. The human mind fills in gaps, jumps to conclusions and often creates monsters out of nothing but its own fears.

PRIMAL FOREST

Forests can be dark forbidding places, home to unknown creatures and easy to get lost in. For our ancestors, who lived before the days of convenient paths and rest-stops, the forest hid enemy attackers and savage predators. Perhaps worst of all was the fear of having an accident and never being found by friends or relatives. Those who wander off the beaten track do so at their peril. 'Whatever you do,' say wise adults in fairy stories, 'don't go into the forest.' On the way to her granny's house, Red Riding Hood forgot to heed her mother's warning and very nearly became a wicked wolf's dinner.

TOOTH & CLAW

This cat is displaying its fangs because it is scared or angry, but the message it sends to the viewer is that it is not a creature to be messed with. Deep down inside us all there is a creature who responds to danger signals such as bared fangs, and whose instinct to run away remains almost irresistible. Fear is our natural safeguard and the impulse to run has saved many lives.

THINGS THAT SHOULD NOT BE

Generation after generation add to the myths and stories of dragons, werewolves, vampires and devils. Eventually, so many stories are told that they take on a life of their own. This creature is obviously a dragon but it has been created by human hands. Many of the monsters that scare us are very human inventions.

NIGHTMARES

When we sleep and our brain goes into neutral gear, random thoughts and things we try not to think about can sometimes bump together to produce nightmares. This picture, *The Nightmare* by Fuseli, combines fears of the dark and the unknown.

CAVE PAINTINGS

Before there were any other means of recording information, our ancestors painted pictures on the walls of their caves. Like all art, the pictures reflected the hopes, dreams, and fears of their creators. This great bison was probably part of a wish-list addressed to the gods. By drawing or symbolizing it on the wall, its creator may have hoped to control his or her fear of a more powerful beast. This may explain our own enthusiasm for horror stories. Talking about, or giving a visible form to what scares us, can help to make it less scary.

 ## FOOD FOR THOUGHT

Monsters do not exist. However, we use them to represent our worst fears and by confronting them we may help ourselves to overcome them. While monsters are not real, our fears certainly are. There might just be something at the window, or sneaking up behind you. There is danger in the woods! There is violence in the world.
It is wise to keep your fear instinct well tuned. Dragons do not exist, but dinosaurs did, and crocodiles still do! Sometimes, fact really is stranger and scarier than fiction.

GLOBAL HAUNTINGS

Although certain places seem to be a focus for supernatural activity, nowhere on Earth is off-limits to ghosts. Wherever there are people, you will find accounts of ghosts. It seems that many ghosts repeatedly act out an action replay of a particular event in their previous life, oblivious to all observers. Others are apparently benevolent and sometimes try to warn strangers of impending danger. However, occasionally ghosts can be malevolent.

SEEING DOUBLE

There are numerous stories of people who apparently have a double and are seen in two places at once. In 1845, in Livaria, Russia, one woman's double image actually appeared alongside her. A school teacher called Madame Sages was able to project an image of herself beyond her body. She used the technique in her classroom to maintain discipline, and while her ghostly image sat in front of the class she would walk around or write on the blackboard. Her actions were witnessed not only by her pupils, but also by her colleagues who eventually asked for her dismissal.

THE SWEET SMELL OF VIOLETS

During the Zulu wars in South Africa in the last century, the Prince Imperial of France was killed. His body was returned to his family for burial and a cairn of stones erected as a memorial on the site where he had died. The following year, the Prince's mother, Eugenie, wished to visit the battlefield where her son had died, but she could not find the memorial. Whilst searching the undergrowth she became aware of the scent of violets, which had been his favourite flower, and was therefore guided to the cairn.

CAR 42, WHERE ARE YOU?

The first Grand Prix to be held in Japan after World War II was in 1963 at the Suzuka circuit in Nagoya. The favourite was Masao Asano driving a car emblazoned with the number 42. During the race, Asano's car went out of control and he suffered a fatal crash. In Japanese the number 42 translates as *shi ni*, which means 'to die'. Racing officials afterwards banned the use of the number 42 but in the following year's Grand Prix event, marshals checking the cars as they passed noticed that a car bearing the number 42 was seen in 8 out of the 25 laps.

CAUGHT IN TIME

In August 1901, two women visiting the Palace of Versailles walked towards the small private château of the queen of France, Marie Antoinette (1755-93). Along the way, they sensed an oppressive atmosphere and passed strangely attired gardeners. A woman was sketching in the garden as they arrived. On a subsequent visit, the layout of the palace and gardens was different and they were convinced they must have slipped back in time on the previous occasion. They later identified the lady sketching as Marie Antoinette. Remarkably, the gardeners and the lady had stared at them, as though they were actually there.

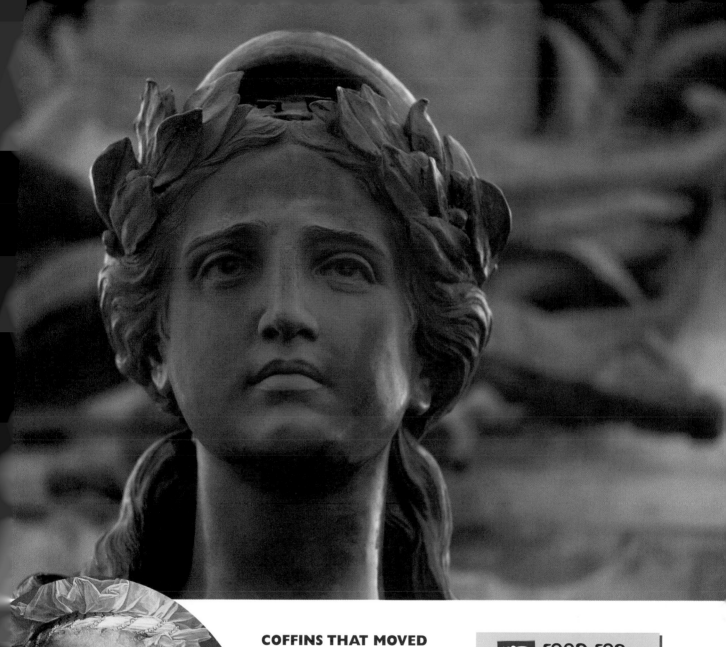

COFFINS THAT MOVED

In 1808, in Christ Church, Barbados, the family crypt of a Mrs Goddard was bought by a plantation-owning family, the Chases. They buried two daughters in the stone tomb, but when it was reopened in 1812 to bury Mr Chase who, like one of his daughters, had committed suicide, the heavy lead coffins inside were found upended. The same happened at two more burials. In 1819, the Governor of Barbados ordered the tomb to be sealed as it was creating fear among the local population. Following noises from within the tomb, it was reopened and the coffins were again in disarray, except Mrs Goddard's. There was no sign of forced entry.

 FOOD FOR THOUGHT

Human intervention could account for many supposed hauntings. In the case of the coffins that apparently moved by themselves, they could simply have been thrown into disarray by surviving relatives of the previous owner of the crypt, who might have resented the intrusion of strangers into the family grave. Tired minds can also create a dream-like state so that we can easily become confused between the real world and that of daydreams, believing that we have seen things when, in fact, there is nothing there.

THIS HAUNTED ISLE

MULTIPLE HAUNTINGS

Many sites in Britain are haunted by more than one ghost. Destroyed by fire in 1939, Borley Rectory in Essex was haunted by several ghosts including a poltergeist, although doubt has now been cast upon their authenticity. Pluckley is said to be the most haunted village in Kent and perhaps in all of England. The most frequently seen ghost is the Red Lady, who haunts the local churchyard shown above, but there are at least a dozen other ghosts that have been reported.

For some reason, the British Isles appear to be the focus of a great deal of supernatural activity. Their populations have recorded more sightings of UFOs, ghosts and other strange phenomena than any other region of comparable size in the world. Every year, there are almost more sightings of ghosts reported in Britain than in the rest of the world put together, making Britain the unofficial ghost capital of the world. Whatever the reasons for this high level of apparent spectral activity, it does mean that there is a wealth of material from all periods of history to investigate.

FEAR OF THE UNKNOWN

Ancient sites, such as the standing stones of Stonehenge in England, are often said to be haunted by spirits that protect their sanctity. One of the most common of these is the Devil himself. It is said that anyone who desecrates the monument will meet an untimely end – perhaps being turned to stone!

THE WHITE LADY

Almost every castle in Britain is said to be haunted, many by unknown spirits. Rochester Castle in Kent is haunted by the ghost of Lady Blanche de Warenne. During a siege of the castle in 1264, she was accosted on the battlements by a rejected suitor, Gilbert de Clare. Ralph de Capo, to whom she was engaged, shot an arrow at her assailant. Deflected by de Clare's armour it unfortunately killed Lady Blanche. Her ghost is now said to walk the battlements every year on the anniversary of her death.

LORE AND ORDER

At Bramshill House in Hampshire, now used as a police training college, there have been so many ghostly encounters that even the worldly-wise police officers have accepted that the house must be haunted. In addition to the more usual ghosts, there are apparently rooms in the house that dogs will not enter and even a path in the grounds that is haunted. One of the more pathetic of the many apparitions that haunt the house is a young girl who accidentally suffocated in a chest during a game of hide-and-seek one Christmas.

 FOOD FOR THOUGHT

Well-known for their fertile imaginations, the British have produced some of the world's greatest works of literature and scientific invention. Perhaps their lively minds are all too willing to see mystery where none exists, embellish it, and pass it on as myth. The often murky weather conditions of the British Isles could account for some of the strange shadowy shapes that are sometimes thought to be ghosts.

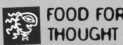
THINGS THAT GO BUMP IN THE NIGHT

Ghosts are often accompanied by strange sounds. Indeed, some ghosts seem only to be audible spirits who never manifest themselves in any visible form. Sounds associated with the Earthly life of the ghost are common; so too is music. Sometimes, especially with poltergeists, a haunting is accompanied by obscene or blasphemous language. This is often voiced through living people, as if the ghost were using them as a vehicle to express its anger. Audible ghosts are often accompanied by a sense of foreboding as if they are predicting some tragic event. In Irish folklore, wailing banshees are female spirits said to warn of an impending death. Such spirits are common in many other cultures, including India and South America.

A PLANE MYSTERY

The American musician Glen Miller is generally held to be the finest band leader of his day. On 15 December 1944, he took a plane from England to Paris to arrange a series of concerts for the US troops in France. The plane disappeared into thick fog and was never seen again. Several reports have described the outline of a small aircraft flying in the area where the plane is believed to have gone down. The sightings are accompanied by the ghostly sounds of a trombone.

THE DEVIL'S MUSIC

In more religious times, ghosts were often seen as the Earthly manifestation of the Devil himself. They were considered to be evil, especially if music accompanied the manifestation. There are many old stories of the Devil attending festivities and disguising himself as a musician to tempt revellers to dance on the Sabbath (seventh day of the week; a holy day). He played demonic music until the dancers either dropped from exhaustion or died.

PLAINTIFF SONG

Mermaids are creatures said to have no soul. In some stories, ghosts are transformed into mermaids and condemned to roam the Earth in search of a soul. Legend tells of the sad, haunting songs these creatures use to lure people to them. There is a theory that these 'ghosts of the sea' are no more than mirages formed by the air distortions caused by differing sea temperatures.

THE DRUMMER OF TEDWORTH

At Tedworth in Wiltshire, England, a famous ghost has been making regular appearances since the 17th century. The ghostly outline of a figure in the full military uniform of the day has often been seen on the old road to Devizes, and heard playing a drum.

SCENTED SPIRITS

Some ghosts make their presence felt by scents and odours, as well as by sound. At Cotehele House in Cornwall, England, several ghosts have been reported over the years, including that of a white lady. Ghostly music is sometimes heard but visitors often ask what the strong herbal fragrance is that seems to permeate the whole house. The scent seems to come and go at random, at all times of the day.

ASTRAL PROJECTION

Most religions believe in a spirit world (or astral plane) to which the souls of the dead return. It is not a separate place in the heavens but is thought to exist all around us at a level of consciousness of which we are normally unaware. The astral body, or spirit of a person, is said to leave the body during sleep and at death, to enter this other level of existence. Ghosts may be astral projections of dead people that have become trapped between this world and the next. Until released in some way, they are unable to pass fully into the spirit world.

FOOD FOR THOUGHT

Maybe victims of violent crimes, such as murder, generate an excess of chemicals such as adrenaline or a high charge of electrical activity within their bodies. In some way this may impart an image or energy field into the surrounding air. Under the right conditions, this image might be seen like a hologram, but it is merely an image with no physical substance.

ISLE OF THE BLESSED

In Celtic mythology, when King Arthur was about to die, he was transported in a boat to Avalon, Isle of the Blessed. According to the legend, Arthur did not die but recovered and would return to fight the enemies of his country whenever he was needed. Unable to rest lest he be called upon, the ghost of Arthur has sometimes been seen at the Cam valley in Somerset, the supposed site of the King's last Earthly battle.

RESTLESS SOULS

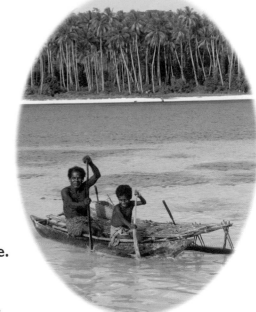

The most common reason given for a ghost manifesting itself is that the spirit or soul of the dead person is troubled and unable to rest. This state of transience is believed to have many causes, but all are in some way connected to a sense of injustice, or perhaps guilt that in life the person did not do all they could have to protect someone. Injustice might be felt by the victim of a violent murder who returns again and again to the scene of the crime, apparently unable to rest until the murderer has been revealed. Alternatively, a ghost might simply be someone who was not ready to die and felt aggrieved that their time on Earth had been cut short.

PHANTOM CARGO

In Papua New Guinea, natives are often seen scanning the horizon for 'phantom cargo'. They wait for dead relatives to come in great canoes (nowadays, ships and planes too) full of goods that will enrich their lives. In the past, missionaries who brought with them artefacts from the civilized world were sometimes allowed to settle in Papua because the natives mistook them for the ghosts of their dead ancestors.

HEADLESS HAUNTINGS

Headless ghosts are common, presumably because the person felt a strong sense of injustice about meeting such a violent end. In the past, the Tower of London was the scene of many executions and is reputed to be the single most haunted building in the world. Similarly, in Paris at the time of the French Revolution (1789-99), the site of the executions is reputedly haunted by several headless ghosts, including Louis XIV and Marie Antoinette.

MYTHICAL GODS

In Nordic mythology, one of the most feared apparitions was Odin, the god of war. Leading a pack of dogs on the 'Wild Hunt', Odin rides across the night sky in search of lost souls. The apparition usually foretold of an impending death.

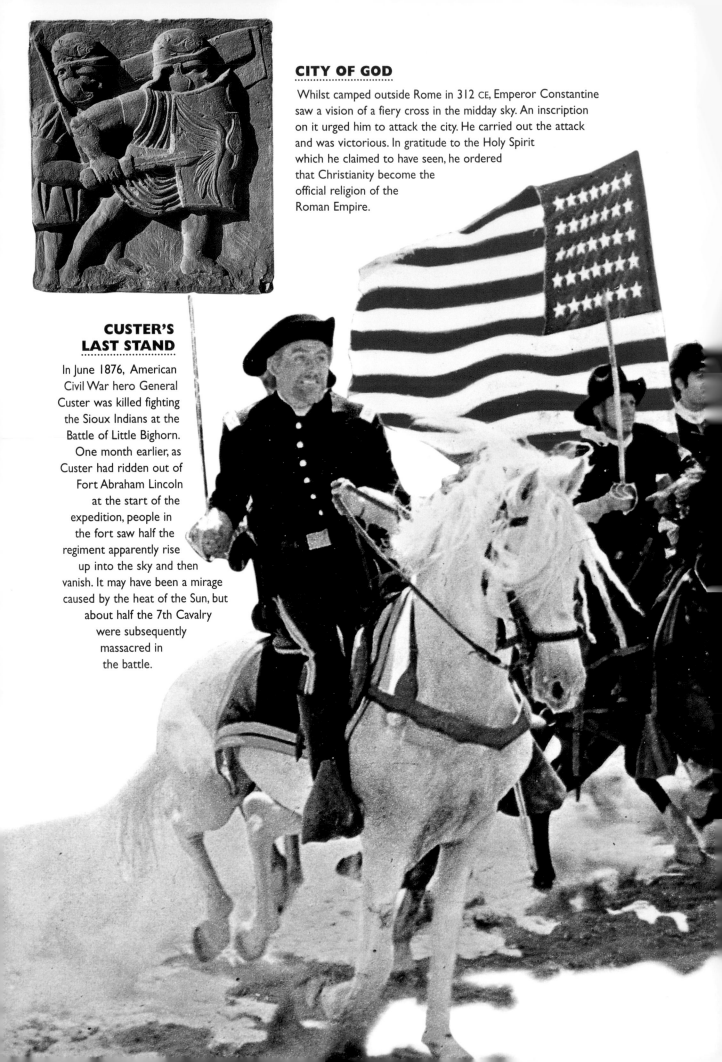

CITY OF GOD

Whilst camped outside Rome in 312 CE, Emperor Constantine saw a vision of a fiery cross in the midday sky. An inscription on it urged him to attack the city. He carried out the attack and was victorious. In gratitude to the Holy Spirit which he claimed to have seen, he ordered that Christianity become the official religion of the Roman Empire.

CUSTER'S LAST STAND

In June 1876, American Civil War hero General Custer was killed fighting the Sioux Indians at the Battle of Little Bighorn. One month earlier, as Custer had ridden out of Fort Abraham Lincoln at the start of the expedition, people in the fort saw half the regiment apparently rise up into the sky and then vanish. It may have been a mirage caused by the heat of the Sun, but about half the 7th Cavalry were subsequently massacred in the battle.

SPECTRAL ARMIES

In the past, when belief in myth and legend was greater than it is today, ghosts tended to be of a more spectacular nature. Visions of gods or heroic figures would appear, and spectral armies fighting battles in the sky were once quite a common occurrence. Today, such visions are rare; in modern hauntings, people tend to see just one ghost. This would seem to indicate a link between the kind of apparition seen and the background and experience of the person who sees it. There are stories of King Arthur and the ancient gods Odin and Thor fighting great ghostly battles. These spectral events could have been mirages of actual battles, while others were perhaps warnings of battles yet to be fought.

DRAKE'S DRUM

Sir Francis Drake (1540-96) used a drum to muster the crew of the *Golden Hind* for battle. According to legend, Drake promised on his deathbed to return and fight for England if ever the drum were beaten at the approach of an enemy. During World War II, stories circulated of warships being miraculously saved from disaster after the ghostly sounds of drumming were heard. However, Drake's drum has never been carried aboard any ship since its return to England in the 16th century.

BOWMEN OF MONS

During World War I (1914-18), the first battle fought by British forces was at Mons in Belgium, where they were grossly outnumbered by the German Army. A report in the newspapers told of a miraculous vision that appeared in the sky above the battlefield, urging on the British troops.

The report claimed the vision was St George and his bowmen, but eyewitnesses from both sides told of an army carrying swords, projected on to the sky like a film. No sounds were heard but the vision was witnessed by many individuals on the battlefield, and has been interpreted by some as divine intervention.

ACTION REPLAY

In August 1942, during World War II, allied troops launched an attack on the German-held town of Dieppe on the coast of Normandy in France. It was a prelude to the D-Day landings and the mission was a success. Nine years later, two women on holiday near Dieppe were woken early one morning by the sound of gunfire. For the next three hours, they listened in stunned silence as the battle of nine years before was re-enacted. Their accounts were afterwards compared to official records of the battle and found to be very similar.

 ## FOOD FOR THOUGHT

The intensity of a life-or-death battle inevitably causes the release of large amounts of adrenaline in the participants. Stories such as the Bowmen of Mons may have been the result of mass hysteria, or born out of a collective memory of some long-past scene. People often see what they want to see. Three different observers of the same event, say a soldier, a priest, and a scientist will each explain it in terms they relate to. The soldier may see an army of ghost soldiers in the sky; the priest the divine light of God; while the scientist may see ball lightning or interpret the others' visions as products of overwrought minds.

UNKNOWN FORCES

Most ghosts appear to be benign and cause no physical harm. However, some spirits seem to be far from passive and can inflict actual bodily injuries or, in extreme cases, death. The most common form of such malevolent behaviour is poltergeist activity. There are also many reports of people falling victim to invisible assailants. One extreme case in 1761 in Ventimiglia, Italy, involved a woman who was attacked by an unseen force. Her body was quite literally torn apart in the presence of her four companions who remained unharmed.

HAIR TODAY, GONE TOMORROW

Between 1876-9 the province of Nanking, in China, suffered a strange yet oddly recurring phenomenon in Chinese history. An invisible assailant ran amok cutting off people's pigtails. Sometimes a shadowy figure was seen, briefly, while at other times the hair was invisibly grabbed from behind and shorn off. Similar happenings were reported in Canada in 1899 and in London in 1922.

POLTERGEISTS

Poltergeist activity often includes objects being hurled through the air, but sometimes they also appear apparently out of nowhere. In 1998, all the items shown here 'fell' into a house in the Northern Territory of Australia within a period of two-three hours. The knife flew past an investigator who was in the house at the time, narrowly missing his ear.

CAUGHT ON CAMERA

This still from 1967 video footage taken in Rosenheim, Germany, shows a light fixture in a solicitor's office swinging unaided. No physical cause could be attributed to the phenomenon. The telephone system also behaved strangely. All four of the office telephones would suddenly ring without reason, and strange power surges were recorded. Sigmund Adam, the solicitor, called in experts to help. The source of these mysterious happenings seemed to be his clerk, a 19-year-old woman. When she left, the activity stopped.

 FOOD FOR THOUGHT

There is plenty of evidence of malevolent poltergeist activity but the source of this 'power' remains a mystery. Much poltergeist activity is centred around young teenage girls at the time when their bodies are undergoing immense physical changes. The girls may themselves be the source of the poltergeist activity, as a result of heightened mental and chemical activity affecting the environment around them.

HOUSE CLEARANCE

The furniture in this house in Dodlestone, Chester, was repeatedly piled into one corner of the room by an unknown force while the owners were out of the room. On one occasion in 1983, computer messages were also received, purportedly transmitted by a man living in the 16th century. Perhaps this is a case of parallel worlds where people from other timespans or dimensions appear to be sharing the same space as ourselves.

BODILY HARM

In 1926, this 13-year-old Romanian girl Eleonore Zugun suffered horrific injuries at the hands of an invisible force. Witnesses describe seeing her throat being squeezed as though she were being throttled. On other occasions, bite and scratch marks appeared spontaneously on her face and neck.

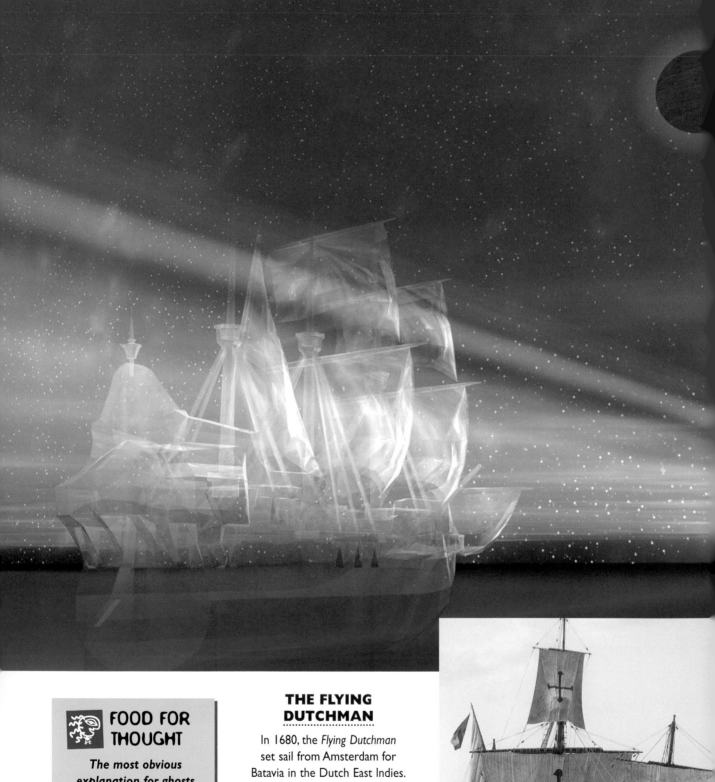

FOOD FOR THOUGHT

The most obvious explanation for ghosts seen at sea is that sailors, subjected to long voyages often in rough waters, can become disoriented or unbalanced. This could distort the sensory perception of seamen and lead them to believe they are actually seeing things that are not there, in much the same way as a hallucination.

THE FLYING DUTCHMAN

In 1680, the *Flying Dutchman* set sail from Amsterdam for Batavia in the Dutch East Indies. The ship was severely damaged in a violent storm off the Cape of Good Hope but the captain refused to turn back. His arrogance and blasphemous behaviour was said to have caused God to condemn him to sail the seas forever. Now considered an ill omen, the phantom ship has since been seen many times, including by the future king of England, George V, in 1881.

PHANTOM SHIPS

Over the centuries, the world's oceans have been the scene of many shipping disasters, and the loss of life has often given rise to tales of ghosts and phantom ships. One area particularly associated with mystery is the Bermuda Triangle in the north Atlantic. Hundreds of ships (and planes) have simply disappeared there without trace and several ghost ships have been reported in the area. When sightings of phantom ships are reported by credible witnesses such as King George V, who as a young naval officer sighted the *Flying Dutchman*, we are forced to take the stories seriously rather than dismiss them as a delusion of sailors who have drunk too much rum.

ALL AT SEA

This rare photograph is believed to show the images of two dead seamen as witnessed by the ship's entire crew. In the 1920s, the oil tanker SS *Watertown* was sailing from the Pacific coast of America to the Panama Canal. Two of the crew died in an accident and were buried at sea. The next day and for several days after, two phantom faces which resembled the dead crewmen were seen in the waves behind the ship. They always appeared in the same position for a few moments, then disappeared. The likenesses appeared during the next two voyages of the ship but were never seen again.

AIR SHIPS

From all corners of the globe there have been reports of mysterious airships; not the great gas-filled zeppelins of the early 20th century, but wooden galleons in full sail drifting across the sky. One such apparition was witnessed in Papua New Guinea in 1959 by the entire staff of a religious mission.

SEA RESCUE

In 1895, Joshua Slocum, the first man to sail round the world single-handed, claimed to have been rescued by a 16th-century ghost. Taken ill during a ferocious storm in the Azores, the American seaman collapsed on his bunk. When he woke, Slocum saw at the helm of his ship, the *Spray*, a seaman who said he was the pilot of the *Pinta*, a caravel (like this replica) that had sailed with Columbus in 1492. The apparition could be dismissed as delirium, except that the *Spray* had remained precisely on course for some 144 km (90 miles).

A VENGEFUL GHOST?

In 1908, the British warship HMS *Gladiator* (left) sank in Portsmouth harbour after colliding with the American steam liner, *St Paul*, with the loss of 27 lives. Incredibly, exactly 10 years later to the hour, the *St Paul* inexplicably capsized in the Hudson River in New York and sank with the loss of four lives. Claims of sabotage were rife but because of the amazing coincidence of date and time, many believed that the ghost of a dead seaman from the *Gladiator* was responsible.

SPIRIT IN THE SKY

It is not uncommon for religious visions or holy spirits to appear in the clouds. This vision of Christ is said to have been photographed during a bombing mission in the Korean War (1950-53). Ghosts are often described as if they are made of the same matter as clouds, and like clouds they can appear for a few moments before vaporizing into thin air. The soul has also been likened to a cloud that vaporizes as it leaves the body.

HEAVENLY VISIONS

From time to time, someone reports seeing a miraculous vision. These visions come in a variety of forms including dreams, ghostly appearances, and miraculous images. In 1980, Mrs Ivy Wilson photographed this rainbow at Woombye in south eastern Queensland, Australia. When she had the film developed she noticed this image of the Virgin Mary and child. The photograph was not taken through glass, so it could not have been a reflection.

HOLY GHOSTS

The Church is usually associated with banishing unwelcome spirits but it also has a fair share of its own ghosts. Many of these apparitions take the form of miraculous images, or visions of Christ, the Virgin Mary or the saints. Apart from these religious visions, the Church tends to explain ghosts as restless spirits whose souls, for one reason or another, are unable to pass over into the afterlife; and they blame the unruly behaviour of poltergeists on the Devil. Most religions classify good and bad spirits in much the same way. The Christian Church calls the spirit of God the Holy Ghost.

GETTING THE HABIT

Everywhere in the world, there are ruined churches or abbeys allegedly haunted by monks and nuns. A Siberian peasant monk, Grigori Rasputin is said to haunt the old royal palace in Moscow. Having gained the confidence of Nicholas II and Alexandra, Rasputin virtually ruled Russia prior to the Revolution. He made many enemies and was murdered by a group of noblemen in 1916. His ghost still walks the corridors of power, supposedly seeking revenge.

METHODIST IN THEIR MADNESS

Towards the end of the 17th century, the Wesley family, founders of the Methodist Church, moved into the Old Rectory at Epworth in Yorkshire, England. The rectory became the centre of much activity and religious fervour. This may have unsettled a Catholic spirit because, for a short period during 1715-16, the house suffered what may have been poltergeist activity. Incidents were many and varied, including a corn grinder and mechanical spit that started up unaided, the sounds of a rocking cradle, mysterious knocking noises and doors that suddenly flew open. Headless animals were seen, and members of the family were hurled against walls. The activity gradually subsided but incidents still occasionally occur there.

DREAMTIME

Aboriginal Australians treat their dead relatives with extreme reverence. They have no fear of death, and the ghosts of their dead are welcome to join in their rituals and celebrations. Aboriginals periodically perform magic rituals to renew their relationship with their dead ancestors who are encouraged to revisit their earthly tribal lands.

FOOD FOR THOUGHT

Seeing visions in cloud shapes has a rational explanation. Known as eidetic images, such visions can be exceptionally vivid but are thought to be recalled from something previously seen. If we stare long and hard at some unrelated surface, many of us will begin to see things such as faces among the patterns on wallpaper or in the flickering flames of a fire, or images in the sky. The human mind works hard to 'read' what is being seen and may eventually interpret abstract shapes as a familiar object or perhaps a desired supernatural being.

LITERARY SPOOKING

GHOST STORIES

Sometimes ghosts were used as a literary device to put across an idea or message, especially in politically sensitive times when the depiction of contemporary events might have been prohibited by a repressive regime. This Japanese woodcut is a piece of veiled war propaganda expressed by having a ghost appear to the Samurai warrior Kingo Chunagon Hideaki during the 19th-century civil wars in Japan.

People who have never seen a ghost find it very hard to believe in them, but many of us keep an open mind about their existence. However, we positively enjoy the inclusion of fictional ghosts in books and plays. A ghostly haunting can be a useful device used by authors to force a character to atone for some misdemeanour. In such plots, the haunted characters usually become so eaten-up by their sense of guilt that they cause their own downfall. These literary ghosts can take on a real and familiar presence in our imagination almost to the point of our believing in them. This may help to keep alive the possibility of ghosts really existing.

GHOULISH GHOSTS

Ghosts are big business. Many films featuring them have drawn huge audiences. Some, like *Casper the Friendly Ghost* (right) and *Ghostbusters,* are light-hearted spoofs, but others, such as *The Exorcist,* are said to be based on real events. *The Exorcist* tells the story of a young girl possessed by the Devil. When the film was shown in a cinema in Australia, several of the audience left before the film had even started because of strange occurrences in the cinema.

GHOSTLY INTERVENTION

Dante's celebrated poem, *The Divine Comedy* may never have been published were it not for the intervention of his own ghost. When he died in 1321, everyone supposed his epic poem was unfinished because, despite an exhaustive search, the missing part of the manuscript could not be found. One night, however, Dante's ghost appeared to his son, Jacopo, in a dream to reveal the secret hiding place. It has been suggested that Jacopo may have finished the poem himself and used the ploy of the ghost to pass off the work as his father's.

GUILTY CONSCIENCE

Many authors have used a ghost in their plots to make their characters face up to the consequences of past actions. In *A Christmas Carol* by Charles Dickens, Scrooge is visited by the ghosts of Christmases past, present and future to make him atone for being a grasping old miser. Shakespeare used a ghost scene to make Macbeth repent his murder of Banquo. Dickens himself was buried at Westminster Abbey in London, yet his ghost is said to haunt a graveyard in Rochester where the author had wanted to be buried.

FOOD FOR THOUGHT

Humankind seems to thrive on mystery. In the past, religions fulfilled our need to explain what we didn't understand. People were afraid of God and believed fervently in demons, evil spirits and the afterlife. Science has explained away many of the mysteries of life and death. Without something outside themselves in which to believe people may feel a spiritual lack. Perhaps being willing to believe in the supernatural is an attempt to fill this void. Also, it is comforting to think there could be some continuance of life after death. Literature and films about ghosts both entertain us and feed an apparent spiritual need, but as far as we know, they have no basis in fact.

GHOSTLY VISIT

The Swiss psychologist Carl Jung (1875-1961) had a great interest in the afterlife and wrote effusively about it in his autobiography. He claimed, among other things, that the ghost of a recently departed friend had visited him in a dream and taken him on a tour of the friend's study. The following day, Jung visited the man's widow and asked to see the study, which he had never seen. To his amazement, it was exactly as he had envisaged in his dream.

GHOSTLY BEASTS

Animals feature quite prominently in accounts of ghost sightings. Sometimes, ghosts of dead pets appear in much the same way as conventional ghosts. Some ghost animals are seen as signals of ill-fortune. Perhaps of more interest is the apparent ability of animals to sense the presence of ghosts before humans are aware of them. This may indicate that animals have a kind of extrasensory perception. Dogs often will not enter a haunted room or, if they do, their hairs will rise as if they detect an intruder. Because animals often possess senses way beyond the normal human range, they may detect the changes to electro-magnetic fields that are often associated with reports of ghosts.

WHITE BIRDS

Although associated with love, peace, and with life itself, white doves are sometimes the signals of impending death. Ghostly white birds have been seen fluttering above the beds of those near to death. Sometimes they are seen by the dying person, at other times by independent witnesses, but they always foretell of a death in the household. Similar sightings have been reported from widely different places such as Ireland and Japan.

FOOD FOR THOUGHT

When confronted by something unexpected, most people react with fear. Large black cats have been seen in locations around the world where such wild animals should not exist. It is all too easy to assume such beasts are in some way supernatural. However, a growing body of evidence suggests that large feral cats, such as black panthers, may have escaped from zoos or private collections and somehow managed to survive in urban areas.

THE DEVIL

Most cultures of the world have their equivalent of the Devil (as he is known in Christianity). He usually represents the opposite of all that is good. To see him is to bring bad luck or death. He often takes the form of a creature who is half man, half beast. Many people believe that all animal ghosts are really the Devil in disguise.

PHANTOM CANINES

The most commonly seen animal phantoms are black dogs which are usually, but not always, associated with evil. They are often believed to be affiliated with the Devil and those who encounter them are frequently injured. Black dog manifestations are also said to predict an impending death. However, it used to be the custom in medieval Europe to bury a dog in new graveyards to protect the souls of the dead.

SACRED RATS

The temple of Karai Ma at Bikaner in the Indian state of Rajasthan is infested with rats. Karai Ma is the goddess of a caste of professional poets, called Charans. Whenever a Charan dies he is believed to return to the temple as a rat, and when a rat dies it is said to return as a poet.

GHOSTLY FELINE

Not all ghostly sightings of animals are of a sinister nature. At a house called King John's Hunting Lodge in Somerset, England, the ghost of a friendly tabby cat (probably the much-loved pet of a previous owner) has often been seen. It appears to enter a first-floor panelled room through a closed door and happily curls up on the floor before disappearing.

SCREECHING OWLS

Owls have traditionally been associated with death. Ghosts of owls that appear at the window of a house and then mysteriously disappear are thought to foretell a death in the family.

A HOUSE BUILT BY GHOSTS

Winchester House in California, was built to appease the spirit world. William Winchester, founder of the famous arms company, died in 1881. His widow, who had recently also lost their only child, became troubled by spirits. A spiritualist told her that the souls of all those killed by a Winchester rifle had banded together to seek revenge. The spirits insisted she build a house to their specifications without rest until she died. In 1884, Mrs Winchester bought a small farmhouse. Day and night for the rest of her life, she expanded it according to the bizarre instructions of the spirits. It has many strange features such as staircases that rise to the ceiling and doors that lead nowhere.

DAY OF THE DEAD

In Mexico, the Purepecha Indians perform elaborate ceremonies not only to venerate the memories of dead ancestors, but also to actively encourage their spirits to appear. In November each year, the dead have divine permission to visit their living relatives during the Day of the Dead celebrations.

 FOOD FOR THOUGHT

Exorcisms are commonly performed by priests of all religions to rid people and places of evil spirits. This could be a simple matter of auto-suggestion (mind over matter). Superstitious people can be possessed by a spirit only because they are willing to believe such a thing is possible. Just as people can convince themselves they are possessed, they can go to a priest in whom they have absolute faith and like-wise convince themselves that the priest is able to exorcise the evil spirit. In reality, they were probably never possessed at all; it was all in their own mind.

GLOBAL ATTITUDES

Cultures around the world have different attitudes to ghosts. Westerners tend to fear ghosts as the restless spirits of the dead, whereas in many supposedly less sophisticated cultures the ghosts of ancestors are celebrated and welcomed. However, if the spirits of the dead are in some way violated they might exact some form of revenge.

In 1942, a man named Adrian Brooks was posted as District Officer at Kasama in what is now Zambia. He inadvertently violated the sacred burial ground of the chiefs of a local tribe, the Wemba, by taking photographs of the site. Witch doctors warned him that he had angered the spirits of their leaders and their ghosts would return to kill him. He scoffed at the warning but three days later he suffered a bizarre fatal accident when a flag pole fell on him.

SPIRIT POSSESSION

In Voodoo ceremonies, participants actively encourage the ghosts or spirits of the dead to possess them. The rhythmic drumming sends dancers into such a frenzy that they go into a trance-like state. The combination of powerful auto-suggestion from the witch doctor and hallucinogenic drugs work together to produce a powerful effect.

DEMONIC POSSESSION

Exorcisms are performed in all religions to banish unwelcome spirits. This Dayak shaman from Borneo in Indonesia is performing an exorcism on an unfortunate individual who has been possessed by a demon.

HALLOWE'EN

In ancient times, 31 October marked the end of the old year when the veil between this world and the afterlife was at its thinnest. On this night, the spirits of the dead were able to leave their graves and wander the Earth. The Christian Church adopted the festival as All hallows' eve and despite its pagan origins the night is still celebrated, especially in America where it involves the light-hearted ritual of 'trick or treat'.

GHOSTBUSTING

CHILL FACTOR

One of the most commonly experienced phenomena during poltergeist activity is a dramatic fluctuation in temperature, as was recorded during an investigation at Mulhouse in France. When ghosts appear, not only is the electro-magnetic field altered, but the ambient temperature can drop by 35°C. No wonder people who see ghosts often report a feeling of cold shivers. Such a drop in temperature can be recorded on portable infrared thermometers.

However sceptical we may be about ghosts, the vast number of reported sightings has encouraged some to take the subject seriously. Scientists have turned their attention to investigating paranormal phenomena, using a growing array of equipment and recording methods. Current research suggests that some form of energy (a by-product of electricity or magnetism) may produce ghostly manifestations. Until more conclusive evidence can be found, however, many will continue to believe in ghosts as supernatural beings from another dimension.

CAUSE AND EFFECT

Ghostly manifestations often occur together with recordable fluctuations in the Earth's electro-magnetic fields. Researchers use special equipment (above) to detect such changes, and some believe that these indicate the presence of ghosts. Others, including scientists at the Laurentian University of Sudbury in Ontario, Canada, believe that natural fluctuations in the Earth's electro-magnetic field can cause the human brain to hallucinate and thus 'create' its own ghosts. If this is true, then sites subject to magnetic fluctuations are likely to seem particularly haunted.

FOOD FOR THOUGHT

Despite the increasing sophistication of modern technology, including photographic and recording equipment, there is no conclusive proof of the existence of ghosts. If they exist, some form of evidence would surely have come to light by now. After all, a vast number of ghosts are claimed to wander the Earth. It seems unlikely that ghosts are the spirits of dead people. Most reported ghosts are probably no more than self-induced images grown out of long-held superstitions.

CAUGHT ON FILM

Some researchers use infrared cameras to detect radiation from spirits, and also to photograph in the dark. More commonly, ghostly figures are unexpectedly caught in a photograph. The example shown here was taken in 1995, during the photographing of a fire at Wem Town Hall, Shropshire. When the picture was developed, this ghostly image appeared. It is thought that this could be linked with a previous fire at Wem in 1677, caused accidentally by a young girl. Critics suggest that such photos are merely accidental double-exposures, reflections, or even blatant frauds.

ARE YOU SITTING COMFORTABLY?

This famous picture of a seance in 1872 shows John Beattie in a trance state, supposedly conjuring up a spirit. However convincing such images may be, not one indisputable photograph of a ghost or spirit has ever been produced. Many mediums have been exposed as frauds, and sceptics believe that seance participants are easily deceived because they see and hear what they choose to.

CLASSICAL MONSTERS

Classical mythology provides us with many scary monsters. Some, which represented supposedly magical forces, were borne out of an ancient awe of natural phenomena such as tidal waves and earthquakes. Others gave a monstrous form to human characteristics, such as the vicious power of gossip personified in the mythical creature called Rumour, a winged creature with a thousand eyes and a thousand ears. Since they are derived from Latin, even the words we use for being scared are rooted in the classical world. A *monstrum* is a warning, a signal, an example of something shocking designed to keep us from straying from the path. Monsters can also be used to scare children into doing as they are told. *Horrere* (to bristle) – that terrible feeling when your hair stands on end – is the Latin word that gave us horror.

CLASH OF THE TITANS

The film *Clash of the Titans* presents a very different version of the legendary Kraken (sea monster). In the film, it is portrayed as a monstrous amphibian very like the city-stomping Godzilla. Here, it is coming to steal away the sacrificial victim Andromeda. In the original legend, a giant whale is sent for Andromeda.

SIRENS

Half woman, half bird, these mythical monsters lured seafarers onto deadly rocks with their beautiful singing. But they were thwarted by Odysseus who filled his crew's ears with wax and tied himself to the mast of his ship so he could not be tempted. The Sirens were eventually destroyed by Orpheus, who sung a sweeter song. Defeated, they flung themselves into the water, where they were turned into rocks.

THE MINOTAUR

A man with the head of a bull – supposedly the result of a curse on Minos, the King of Crete – the minotaur lived in the centre of a great maze. Each year, the Athenians had to send seven boys and seven girls to be sacrificed to the minotaur, or risk invasion. The minotaur was eventually slain by Theseus, a Greek hero who went in disguise as one of the sacrificial victims. Theseus fell in love with Ariadne, the daughter of the King of Crete, who gave him a sword and a roll of string by which he could retrace his steps through the maze.

HYDRA

The hero Hercules was told to defeat the hydra, a snake-like monster with nine heads. Each time he struck off one of the heads with his club, two more would grow in its place. But Hercules managed to burn away eight of the heads before burying the ninth (which was immortal) under a rock.

MEDUSA

The Gorgons were three terrifying creatures who had snakes instead of hair, as well as wings, claws, and enormous teeth. Two of them, Stheno and Euryale, were immortal, but the most famous was the mortal Medusa. Once a beautiful girl, she was turned into a monster by the jealous Greek goddess, Athena. Medusa became so ugly that one look at her face would turn men into stone. The hero Perseus defeated her by looking only at her reflection. He was then able to cut off her head. But even after death, the sight of her ugliness continued to turn anyone who looked upon her into stone.

ELIZABETH BÁTHORY

Stoker's Count Dracula may have been a composite character inspired by Vlad the Impaler and Countess Báthory. Arrested in 1610 for murdering young girls, she believed bathing in the blood of her victims would keep her looking youthful.

 FOOD FOR THOUGHT

The idea of vampires is really fairly silly, but they do combine several important elements. There's the historical aspect, and the fear of a powerful individual who abuses those less fortunate than himself. But, ultimately, vampire stories are rooted in a fear of the dead and in the observation of what happens after people die. Their skin shrinks back slightly, making teeth and nails look longer; they become pale as if their blood has been drained away. A wolf or a bat is just an animal, but say it's possessed by a dead soul and you have a scary story. And a cloud of gas! Might this be methane gas rising over a graveyard from a decaying body beneath the earth? There's a rational explanation for everything except perhaps why people find these stories so compelling.

VAMPIRES

Supposedly the ghost of a heretic (a person who holds different beliefs to those of the established Church) or a criminal, a vampire comes out of its grave at night in the guise of a bat to suck blood from people as they sleep. As a result, the victims become vampires. The most famous vampire is from the novel *Dracula* (1897) by Bram Stoker. Count Dracula was based on two historical figures but legends of vampirism existed long before the book was written. Some myths say vampires cannot be reflected in a mirror because they have no soul. Also, old mirrors were made with silver and, since Jesus was betrayed for 30 pieces, silver was thought to reflect evil.

MODERN VAMPIRES

Modern myths say vampires can change into wolves, bats, or even clouds of gas. They have long fangs for sinking into human flesh and drinking blood, and they have to stay out of sunlight. They can only be killed by a stake through the heart.

VLAD THE IMPALER

Vlad V of Walachia (1456-1476) was born in 1431 in Transylvania. He was a brutal warlord reputed to have killed over a hundred thousand people. Stories tell of him nailing hats to people's heads, skinning them alive and, most famously, impaling them on upright stakes – for which he earned the nickname Vlad the Impaler. He was also called Vlad, son of the dragon (or Dracula). His behaviour made some people think he had sold his soul to the Devil, and led to rumours that he would never be admitted into Heaven. Murdered in 1476, his tomb was reported empty, and the legends began.

THE VAMPIRE BAT

This humble bat scrapes a hole in an animal's skin and drinks its blood. In that sense, it is little different from a mosquito (just bigger), but the blood-drinking was associated with vampirism and the name stuck.

KALI

Kali, the Hindu goddess of death is one of the most fearsome creatures of mythology. Even today, animals are sacrificed to her, but in the past it was human beings who were offered to appease her anger. She is usually depicted as a black-skinned, red-eyed demon with four arms, wearing a necklace of skulls. The Indian city of Calcutta is said to derive from kali-ghat, the 'staircase of Kali' which her worshippers use to enter the River Ganges.

GARGOYLES

Originally simple spouts for draining water from the roofs of churches, gargoyles (French for gullet is *gargouille*) were carved into a variety of grotesque stone demons. In the 7th century a great dragon called Gargouille was believed to live in the River Seine in Paris.

DEMONS & DEVILS

The Hindu deva and the Greek daemon, are both creatures of myth that have been changed over time into our words devil and demon. Once simple paranormal beings of both good and bad nature, they were proclaimed as wholly evil with the ascendence of Christianity. The Christian term Satan comes from the Hebrew word shatana which means adversary. In the Bible, Satan is identified in Revelations as meaning the same thing as the Dragon and the Serpent. In other words: the Devil. Satan is the supreme evil spirit; the enemy and tempter of man and the ruler of Hell.

PAN

Half man, half goat, the ancient Greek god Pan became a model for many Christian images of the Devil. The cloven hooves and the horns seem to have been carried over into the modern idea of the Devil. We get our word *panic* from the terrible fear his appearance was intended to strike into non-believers.

FALLEN ANGELS

Biblical angels may do the bidding of God, but in the *Old Testament*, this often meant laying waste to armies, killing children and striking people down with diseases. John Milton linked this with the idea of Lucifer, and wrote the book *Paradise Lost*, a tale of Lucifer's expulsion from Heaven. The ousted angel and his followers prefer to be rulers in Hell than servants in Heaven.

LUCIFER

'How art thou fallen from Heaven, O Lucifer, star of the morning,' said the Bible's *Book of Isaiah*, poetically linking the death of the King of Babylon with the arrival of the morning star, Venus (*lucifer*: light-bringer). Over time, this phrase was confused with Satan himself, and the name Lucifer came to be identified with evil.

 FOOD FOR THOUGHT

What great stories. If people at war pretend their enemies are inhuman (to avoid admitting they are committing murder) the tales of ancient wars can fast become tales of demonic attacks. Like the Sirens of Ancient Greece, demons and devils are simply symbols of evil and temptation, perhaps even of past enemies. Blaming a devil for a wicked deed seems easier than taking responsibility for it.

GOBLINS, KOBOLDS & SPIRITS

FROM DJINNI TO GENIE

Middle Eastern *djin* (demons) were thought to have been created from fire 2,000 years before Adam was made out of clay. They entered Western mythology as genies, although their original destructive powers have been tempered over time to offer little more than the granting of wishes.

FOOD FOR THOUGHT

Some real people are born small – the average height of the Congo Mbutsi tribe is a mere 137 cm (4 ft 6 in) – but they have no relation to the mythical beings shown here. It is said that elves and fairies are wounded by iron. This may refer to the local peoples of Bronze Age culture being pushed into the forests and wilderness by invading Iron Age tribes. Other fairy tales seem to be remnants of pagan religions, belittled by the arrival of Christianity and mutated as they were passed by word of mouth through the generations.

Ultimately, the simplest explanation works best – if you can't think of a good reason for some act of mischief, blame an evil spirit. Of course, mischief-makers have to be small; if they were giants, everyone else would have seen them, too. The sound of mice scurrying behind the walls may have added credence to the ancient legends.

Perhaps with their origins in the desire of children to have something smaller than themselves in the world, the little people are another kind of monster. Sometimes demonic, they are more often impudent or mischievous rogues who dwell in our houses, chinks in trees, and other nooks and crannies. The mythologies of most cultures include stories of little people such as gnomes, goblins, kobolds, and leprechauns. They were often portrayed as misshapen old men who hoarded treasure. The most famous are perhaps the Scandinavian Norse dwarves. They had their own king, were not unfriendly to humans, but could be very vindictive or mischievous. The Norse word 'alfar' may have given us the English word 'elf'.

DWARVES

According to Norse mythology, dwarves began their existence as maggots in the flesh of a giant. Found in the mythology of most races, they were said to live beneath the earth, or in rocks, and to be guardians of its precious metals and stones. Dwarves were sometimes believed to help human beings. Carved on this stone tomb, four dwarves are depicted supporting the sky over a dead Viking.

KOBOLDS

Another kind of dwarf said to live in German mines were Kobolds, who did everything they could to make life difficult for silver miners. They would cause cave-ins, explosions and rockfalls. Miners lived in dread of their activities. Sometimes, they mixed silver ore with their own magic metal and this became known as *cobalt*.

FAIRIES

We think of fairies as the tiny butterfly-like creatures we know from Victorian children's stories. But in earlier times they were something to be afraid of – roaming creatures said to steal babies from their mothers' arms. Fairies began as inhabitants of the dark forests, creatures who would lure unsuspecting travellers to their doom. In the Middle Ages, they were symbols of temptation; they lured people to commit sin without revealing that there would be a horrible price to pay.

ELVES

Although sometimes allies of humans, elves were notoriously unreliable, always likely to go back on bargains and twist the words of promises. In the Middle Ages when a child was born dead or disabled it was believed that fairies or elves had swapped the human child for one of their own – a changeling. It is often said that elves are hurt by iron, a metal said in China to 'wound the eyes of dragons'.

FOOD FOR THOUGHT

There is an element of truth in these stories. Some people do grow to be very tall, but that doesn't make them monsters. Tall people often suffer from a variety of ailments, including bad backs, stoops and tunnel vision. The latter may explain why Goliath did not notice a rock flying at him from the side. But what about the really big giants of legend? Many are folktales that grew out of the need to explain strange natural phenomena. Most, as usual, are products of the human mind. In the earliest days of childhood, we are loomed over by adults so much taller than we are that to a tiny child they could seem like giants.

GOLIATH

A huge champion of the Philistines in the Bible, Goliath was defeated by a stone slung at him by David, the future king of Israel. He was said to stand 2.75 metres (9 ft) high or, according to another source, 1.8 metres (6 ft) high – the difference between a tall story and a tall man.

REAL-LIFE GIANTS

In this photo, these two towering men are stood on either side of a tiny Professor Ricalton in Kasmir, but how *giant* are they? Perhaps the professor is actually quite short – the 'giants' are much taller than average but not excessively so. People of great height are not unheard of but the picture is oddly posed. Professor Ricalton has taken his hat off; while the two 'giants' wear turbans that make them look taller. The image is impressive, but parts of it are cosmetic – rather like a puffer fish that pretends to be bigger than it is. Great size or the illusion of it is used in the natural world to scare away potential predators.

GIANTS

At the opposite end of the scale from little people are the giants. The idea of giants is probably based on physical reality, since some people are just very tall. The average height of the Tutsi people of Rwanda/Burundi is 1.8 metres (6 ft). The world's tallest man on record is Robert Wadlow who was 2.7 metres (8 ft 11 in) when he died in 1940. Wadlow was a midget compared to the giants who are used to scare us in mythology, such as Atlas who held the entire world in his hands; the Giant of Mont St Michel slain by King Arthur; and the Gigantes, a race of giants said by the Greeks to be imprisoned in volcanoes. Our ancestors may have found it more reassuring to believe a volcanic eruption was the work of giants than to think they were living on a ball of fire. Large natural phenomena such as the Giant's Causeway, said to be the ruins of a road built between Ireland and Scotland, were sometimes seen as proof of the existence of giants.

CYCLOPS

Said by legend to be the builders of great prehistoric walls to be found in parts of Greece and Italy, the Cyclops were a race of one-eyed giants, thought to enjoy the taste of human flesh. They often featured in the tall tales of seafarers. Ulysses (Odysseus), mythical king of Ithaca in Greece, and Sinbad the Sailor both reported encounters with them.

GIANT THREATS

Some giants are designed to make people feel small and vulnerable. This huge foot is one piece of what was an enormous statue of the Roman emperor (306-37 CE), Constantine the Great. It was deliberately built to extreme proportions to remind the people who was boss.

VOODOO

Voodoo began in the beliefs of the African slaves of the 1800s, who were taken to work on French plantations in the New World. They believed sorcerers had the power to control zombies (the living dead). But zombies weren't really dead at all, they were people who had been fed a soup of the datura tree. It sedated them, slowing their heart-rate so they only appeared to be dead.

FRANKENSTEIN & THE LIVING DEAD

Many religions believe we all have a soul, and the human body is merely a vessel to carry around our consciousness. Myths about the afterlife often start with the question: what happens to someone when they die? The body may stop working but, so argue the religions, the soul goes somewhere else. A soul without a body is a ghost. So what is a body without a soul?

KURU

Cannibals of the South Pacific used to eat the brains of their enemies in order to gain their powers. Unfortunately, eating human flesh (especially brains) is liable to pass on some terrifying diseases, including kuru, the laughing sickness. The infected person went mad, supposedly possessed by evil spirits – another version of the living dead. And, once this enemy was defeated, the conquerors would eat his brain and catch the disease too.

GALVANI'S EXPERIMENTS

In 1791, the Italian scientist Luigi Galvani discovered that by passing electricity through the legs of a dead frog, he could make them twitch. It led to the supposition that electricity could bring the dead back to life. Because electricity seemed so mysterious, some people thought it must be the divine force that gave life to dead things.

FOOD FOR THOUGHT

There's no arguing with Galvani's experiments. The same process is used to this day to jump-start failed hearts in hospital crash-carts. The Frankenstein story is rooted in a fear of science at a time when there were stories of doctors robbing graves so they could study the corpses. As for the restless dead, see the notes on vampires (pages 36-37). Modern-day afflictions such as schizophrenia or catatonia may have been interpreted in the past as possession by demons or living death. Kuru remains a fascinating topic for the modern scientist. Mad Cow Disease can pass to humans from eating the brains or spinal columns of infected cattle. Just think how much more dangerous the human variation must have been.

DAWN OF THE DEAD

Modern horror films take the zombie legends of other cultures and put a Christian spin on them. They claim that because Hell is full, some souls are waking up back in the bodies they are supposed to have left behind. Some films feature the zombies embarking on a quest for human brains; a strange craving which takes its inspiration from the kuru myths.

FRANKENSTEIN'S CREATURE

In Mary Shelley's Gothic novel published in 1818, Frankenstein was the mad professor who made a monster with bits and pieces of several dead bodies sewn together and reanimated with electricity from lightning. But was it human? If a dead body is reanimated, does it have a soul?

NATURAL MONSTERS

KILLER FISH

The piranha shoal is another monstrous fear. A single fish is ugly but relatively harmless. An entire school of these sharp-toothed creatures can strip the flesh from a creature in the water within seconds. In Brazil in 1981, more than 300 people were eaten alive by piranhas when a boat capsized near Obidos.

Not all monsters are figments of the human imagination. Perhaps the most fearsome creatures to have lived were the dinosaurs. Fortunately, these prehistoric monsters never shared the Earth with us; they died out some 65 million years ago, long before we arrived. But the natural world still has plenty of other fierce creatures to inspire a sense of the monstrous in mankind. The ancestry of some, such as crocodiles, can be traced back to the Mesozoic Era when dinosaurs lived. Were we to encounter these creatures roaming free in their natural habitat, the potential dangers facing us would be very real.

TYRANNOSAURUS REX

The most famous of the dinosaurs, this enormous, meat-eating predator was genuinely fearsome. Up to 14.5 metres (47 ft) long and 6 metres (20 ft) high, it weighed almost 7 tonnes (8 tons) and boasted fangs 15 cm (6 inches) long. These awesome creatures terrorized east Asia and North America but, luckily for us, the last tyrannosaur died millions of years before the arrival of humanity.

 FOOD FOR THOUGHT

Are there real-life mammoths in Siberia? The 'evidence' has probably come from dead mammoths only recently dug out of ancient ice. In the 13th century, Genghis Khan turned a herd of elephants loose on the Russian steppes. It is unlikely that any of their descendants live undiscovered today, and even less likely is the survival of mammoths! The way all these creatures are so different to us makes us see them as monstrous. Their teeth, their savage speed, their reptilian origins, all scare us, but they are not monsters. Lions only hunt for food; the crocodile has no interest in human affairs; and no tyrannosaur ever declared war or committed a crime. Only humans have fought to master the natural world. As part of nature, perhaps our greatest fear is that by harming its creatures, we may one day harm ourselves.

MAMMOTHS

Elephants are large and scary enough. Imagine if they had extra long tusks and were hairy. The bodies of prehistoric mammoths have been found in the ice of Siberia and the local tribesmen have been known to take the tusks to sell as ivory. Some people in remote parts of Russia have reported seeing live mammoths but their stories are difficult to substantiate.

THE KING CHEETAH

Thought for many years to be nothing more than a ghost story, this huge predator with a tiger-like stripe down its back has been known to carry off people along the Mozambique border. Called a *mngwa* by the locals, rumours of its existence were proved true when Paul and Lena Bottriel photographed the 'king' cheetah in 1975.

CROCODILE TEARS

Around 2,000 people a year fall prey to salt-water crocodiles. Left over from prehistory, crocodiles have been hunting by the riverside for eons. They are not natural enemies of man because, in fact, they have been around far longer than the human race. If we invade their natural habitat it is our own fault if they attack us, yet we have demonized these creatures.

THE LION'S SHARE

Today, lions and tigers are familiar to us from television and zoos. But in the wild, before the days of guns and traps, these big cats were greatly feared. Wise humans left them well alone, even though a lion would only attack a human being if it was provoked. Like many so-called *monsters* of the world, they are more likely to be afraid of us than we are of them.

DRAGONS

SNAKES IN THE GRASS

The serpent is a symbol of evil in many cultures. See the forked tongue, a symbol of telling lies, and hence of evil and deception.

The dragon is the super-monster of many cultures, and is born of a mixture of many different creatures. The Chinese legend of the birth of the dragon was that as tribes with different animal totems united they produced a composite creature with the antlers of a deer, the body of a snake, the wings of a bird (and so on). Eventually, they had invented a creature like no Earthly beast. In Chinese, the word dragon is also used to describe waterspouts and tornadoes, which reinforces the idea of a dragon as an unstoppable force of nature. The American Indians created their own equivalent in their Thunder Lizard legends, inspired by their discovery of dinosaur bones – they could not have known that these creatures had been dead for millions of years. Once again, these are examples of the human mind fleshing out monsters created largely in the imagination.

THE EVIL SERPENT

Western dragons have their origins in the Greek *drakon* meaning serpent. More likely to be dangerous (Chinese dragons are just tough), Western dragons have become the personification of evil and of the Devil himself (notably, the serpent in the Garden of Eden). Here, Saint George defeats 'the dragon'. Some other pictures depict the dragon as a human figure.

FOOD FOR THOUGHT

Until causes are understood, humankind creates monsters to explain fearful events such as tornadoes, waterspouts and earthquakes. The Komodo Dragon is called a dragon, yet it doesn't fly nor breathe fire. If you call a pet hamster Dragon, it doesn't make him one.

EARTHQUAKES

On the rare occasions in the past when our ancestors found dinosaur fossils, they did not know how to explain them. Some assumed that the bones were of giant creatures who lived in the bowels of the Earth. When one of the sleeping giants shivered, the whole Earth would quake.

THUNDER & LIGHTNING

In China, the word for *dragon* was also used to describe thunder and lightning flashing in the sky. This helps to explain the longer, snakelike shape of the oriental dragon. To an ancient Chinese sage, this picture would show two dragons fighting in the sky. Storms weren't the only natural phenomena attributed to the work of dragons, however. Offshore tornadoes that whisked water into great whirling spouts were known as sea dragons. This meant that matter-of-fact reports of bad weather could have been misunderstood as attacks by supernatural creatures.

ORIENTAL DRAGONS

East Asian dragons are normally good-natured. As long as they are respected, they can act with great kindness. According to some stories, a great person may become an immortal or a spirit. After many centuries, the spirit becomes a dragonet and dives beneath the earth to sleep. When it finally wakes as a dragon, it tears itself free and flies up to heaven.

A REAL DRAGON

In 1912, a 3-metre (10-ft) lizard that ate pigs and goats was discovered in the islands of the Indian Ocean. It was immediately dubbed the Komodo dragon, as it is still called today. In 1979, an expedition to New Guinea found archaeological evidence of an even bigger lizard. Perhaps a live specimen is still waiting to be discovered.

LAKE MONSTERS

Places as far afield as Sweden, Ireland, New Zealand, Africa, and Russia have their own mysterious monsters. In Iceland there is the Lágarfljótsormur, in the North American Lake Champlain there is Champ, and in Canada there is Manipogo, the monster of Lake Winnipeg. Far from being one of a kind, it would seem that Scotland's Loch Ness monster has many cousins around the world.

This convincing picture was taken on Loch Ness in 1977. But is it a monster's head or a branch?

NESSIE

Ever since 565 CE, when Saint Columba ordered a creature in the loch to leave humans alone, the Loch Ness monster has been one of the most famous beasts of Scottish folklore. Often presumed to be a throwback to the time of the dinosaurs, Nessie is said to have either a long neck on a large body, or to be an eel-like shape, depending on who is telling the story.

FOOD FOR THOUGHT

Many of the lake-monster sightings have been discredited as hoaxes or proved to be something mundane like ducks, a swimming dog with a stick, or simply the wind blowing on the water. It is true that some prehistoric creatures may have survived in the vastness of the oceans, but the chances are remote of any remaining in the relatively tiny area of a lake. These things are not immortal; they would need others to breed with. There wouldn't be just one monster, but several per location. If they exist, surely we would have indisputable evidence by now.

Does Nessie have humps? This picture taken in 1951 by Lachlan Stuart would seem to suggest so. Or, are they just rocks?

OGOPOGO

In the Canadian province of British Columbia lies Lake Okanagan, where the native Okanakane Indians have always said there was a monster. They called him *Na-ha-ha-itkh*, and would throw a meat sacrifice into the lake whenever they crossed it. Known for its humps, its snakelike appearance and its thick body, Ogopogo is often sighted but has never harmed anyone in living memory. Ogopogo even had a song written about him in the 1920s: *His mother was an earwig, his father was a whale, a little bit of head, and hardly any tail, and Ogopogo was his name.*

RRIERE

6 Agosto 1961

...a venuta da lontano

...itchcock - a pagg. 5 e 7

ISSIE

This is a model of Issie, the monster rumoured to live in the depths of Lake Ikeda in Japan. Like Nessie, it has never been known to harm humans and seems to be very camera shy. Though many people have *almost* photographed it, a conclusive picture has yet to appear.

LAKE IKEDA, JAPAN

A lake just waiting for a monster. This inexplicable ripple could mean Issie is about to surface.

SEA MONSTERS

TEMPEST

As late as the Elizabethan era (1558-1603), large areas of the globe remained uncharted. When Shakespeare wrote *The Tempest*, he was inspired by tales of monsters and shipwrecks that had circulated from the New World (the Americas). For the people of pre-modern times, monsters such as this were thought to be lurking just outside mapped areas. Any journey was a journey into the unknown, and into fear.

Two-thirds of the Earth is covered by water. Although we know most of the land well there are still unexplored areas of the deep sea that remain a mystery. History is rich with stories of sea monsters. Sailors told tales of many extraordinary creatures, such as the now legendary mercreatures who were said to have the body of a human and the tail of a fish. What the sailors had seen were probably dolphins, narwhals or dugongs. Perhaps they had been at sea too long or had had an extra tipple of rum before going on watch. But not all the sightings were quite so fanciful. Until 1938, coelacanths were thought to have become extinct some 50 million years ago. It is now known that a small number of coelacanths live in very deep water off the African coast. If they have survived for millions of years, other prehistoric 'monsters', such as the megalodon, a 30-metre (100-ft) shark, may also still be cruising about in the unexplored depths of some ocean.

 FOOD FOR THOUGHT

The thought of a whale shark is very scary, but it isn't a monster. Neither is a shark. We invade their territory, not the other way around. The whales and sharks of ancient tales probably grew in the telling to give us the sea monsters from the past, but there's no arguing with some of the evidence. Nine-metre (30 ft) squid have been found and studied by scientists and, if the scars on the sperm whales are anything to go by, they could well be the babies. No one knows how big a full-grown giant squid might be.

FANGTOOTH

This scary-looking fish is actually quite small, and unlikely to turn up anywhere near people because it lives miles down in the sea. On the rare occasions when it is washed up on shore, such teeth might scare humans into imagining what a giant version would look like.

OCTOPI

The octopus has always intrigued seafarers. With its eight arms, its suckers and its powerful hidden beak, it is one of the strangest creatures of the deep. As stories grow with the telling, many have speculated on the existence of giant octopi large enough to swallow a man whole.

GIANT SQUID

Thought to be the stuff of legend, the giant squid (or kraken) may well exist. The first people to discuss it were the crews of the whaling ships in the 19th century. Some whales they killed had the scars of giant suckers on them, as if they had survived a battle. F.T. Bullen reported a harpooned sperm whale vomiting thousands of squid (its traditional diet). Also among the debris were huge bits of tentacle as thick as a man's body. This 19th century Japanese print shows a giant squid as one of the legendary Dragon King's faithful army.

WHALES

The great size of whales has always struck dread into the hearts of sailors, but these peaceful creatures have no interest in harming humanity. Their value as food and for raw materials in candles and corsets (among other things) meant that they have been hunted to the brink of extinction. But whales must have been terrifying for early whalers who had nothing but spears to throw.

SHARKS

Sharks are our modern-day sea monsters, but not because sharks are evil (although, like this blue shark, some do look evil). Unless provoked, most sharks will leave humans alone. The biggest known fish in the world is the whale shark – a huge 18 metres (60 ft) long, but it doesn't eat people, just tiny plant and animal organisms called plankton.

WERE- CREATURES

A true were-creature is half man, half beast. From early prehistoric cave paintings we can see that primitive shamans were thought to have the power of shape-shifting. Similar stories were told of the Vikings, who often wore wolf skins to strike fear into their enemies. In modern mythology, such as the film *I Was a Teenage Werewolf*, werewolves have been given an additional dimension: the teenager boy's monstrous fear of never being loved, of having a dark side that cannot be tamed, of being a rebel without a cause, or a beast in search of a beauty to tame him.

THE FULL MOON

Werewolves supposedly take on their beastly shape at the full moon, when supernatural powers are at their greatest.

FOOD FOR THOUGHT

The idea of changing into a wolf (or in some cultures into tigers, bears, or lions) shows a natural human fear of the monstrous. It symbolizes leaving the safety of civilization and plunging back into the past to become the very thing our ancestors sought to hide from – our own animal nature. As with the shape-shifting vampire, some people may have been malevolently motivated to blame the random attack of a wild animal on an enemy disguised as a monster. The pictures here are not of werewolves, they're just plain wolves! And someday we'll wake up and notice that the better-lit nights of the full moon make it easier for humans to commit nocturnal crime, especially in the past when there was no street lighting.

THE WOLF OF THE WILD

Mankind has always had an uneasy relationship with the wolf. Some time in the distant past, a branch of the wolf family became 'man's best friend' but wolves, closely related to dogs, have remained fierce creatures. Although they are feared for hunting in packs, they would not attack humans unless provoked by them.

THE FRENCH WOLF

Thought to be a werewolf, the beast of Gévaudan terrorized the French countryside for three years between 1764 and 1767. Said to be the size of a cow, it claimed the lives of over 60 peasants by the time it was killed – shot in the chest by a silver bullet. Its stomach was said to contain the collar bone of a young woman, but its carcass was buried and has never been found.

ANCIENT WOLVES

Ancient writers talked of *lycanthropy*, *kuanthropy* and *boanthropy*, conditions of madness in which afflicted persons believed themselves to be a wolf, a dog, or a cow. In Northern Europe, similar tales were told of men who turned into bears, and in Africa, hyenas.

The Greek historian Herodotus (c. 480-425 BCE) claimed the Neuri people of Sarmatia (north east Europe) were sorcerers: 'For each Neurian changes himself once a year into the form of a wolf, and continues in that form for several days, after which he resumes his former shape.'

BEAUTY & THE BEAST

The tale of a man who looks
(and often behaves) like an
animal is not limited
to werewolves.
It also crops up
in *The Strange Case
of Dr Jekyll and Mr Hyde*
(1886), and in the fairy tale of
Beauty and the Beast. The stories tell
of savage creatures who menace beautiful girls
– timeless representations of
mistrust between men
and women.

HAIRY MEN
OF MANDALAY

Don't believe humans can
get that hairy? A disease
called hypertrichosis can cause
excessive facial hair, as in this
photograph of hairy men of
Mandalay. Since our distant ape
ancestors had hair all over, it is
only relatively recently in human
history that we began to lose
our all-over fur.

THE YETI

The Abominable Snowman, or Yeti, is perhaps
the most famous ape-like creature. It may be
a distant, ape-like, relative of man. The people
of the Himalayas believe it exists, and the
mountain range is so remote it is possible that
undiscovered creatures do live there. In 1975, a
Polish hiker called Janusz Tomaszczuk claimed
he had been approached by an ape-like creature
in the Himalayas. His screams drove it away.

THE SCOTTISH SNOWMAN

This photograph
was taken high up
on Ben Nevis, the
highest mountain in
the British Isles. Is it
the Scottish equivalent
of the Yeti? Or just a
man in a gorilla suit?

YETI'S FOOTPRINTS

Nobody has ever captured
a Yeti, but its footprints
have been photographed.
These deep, large footprints
are spaced wide apart and
suggest a tall, heavy
creature. It certainly isn't
human. But it might be the
elusive Tibetan blue bear, a
creature that has not been
seen alive by Westerners
but whose skins have been
sold to museums.

GREAT APES

Like the werewolf, what scares us most about the great apes is how like and yet how different they are to us. The gentlest of the great apes, the mountain gorilla, was regarded as a fanciful invention of storytellers until the early years of the 20th century. Perhaps the stories of the Himalayan Yeti, the American Big Foot or the Russian Alma are equally well founded.

KING KONG

A classic horror film tells the tale of King Kong, a 15-metre (50-ft) prehistoric great ape who is captured, taken to New York and put on display. He escapes and terrorizes the city before finally falling to his death from the Empire State Building. His climactic rampage through the city was the result of human intervention, which made his death all the more tragic.

BIG FEET

If this 1995 Big Foot photograph is a fake, it means someone has been crazy enough to make false Big Foot tracks running for several miles in remote parts of the US and Canada.

BIG FOOT

In 1967, Roger Patterson took this famous film of an ape-like figure in Northern California. Its height is estimated at 2 metres (6 ft 5 in). Could *Pithecanthropus Erectus*, a species of primitive man believed to be extinct, still live in remote parts of the world?

FOOD FOR THOUGHT

There may yet be more creatures for us to discover in the wilderness. The existence of a Scottish apeman is doubtful, but Canada and the Himalayas are large enough to allow for the possibility of undiscovered life. Since mountain gorillas exist, there's a chance that the Yeti could too. Or perhaps Big Foot? Both these great apes are reputed to live in wastelands devoid of human habitation and would probably be more scared of us than we are of them.

SCARING YOUR ENEMIES

This suit of Japanese samurai armour is designed to look monstrous. In the heat of battle, warriors needed all the help they could get. Horned helmets or even spiked armour for their horses all helped to terrify their enemies.

GRENDE

In the Old English epic tale of *Beowulf*, Grendel was the troll-like creature who plagued King Hrothgar's hall for 12 years. Eventually, Grendel was slain by Beowulf, the hero who wrestled with him and tore off his arm. Grendel's mother came seeking vengeance for her son and proved to be an even more dangerous ener

FAMILY FORTUNES

In the Middle Ages, few people could read and write. Noble families and public figures therefore needed a recognizable mark to symbolize and display their power. The family's mark was made into a seal to authenticate legal documents, and was also used on buildings, flags and armour. These marks often included powerful beasts such as lions or bears. Noble families often combined in the same way as prehistoric tribes. This combination meant new heraldic beasts had to be created that included different parts from each family's coat of arms. These new non-existent creatures became symbols of larger more powerful families.

HERALDIC BEASTS

Noble families often regarded their family symbols as guardian spirits, or designed them to strike fear into their enemies.

GRIFFIN

The Griffin is part eagle, part lion. These two heraldic symbols are a sign of power and strength – and combined they make a scary monster indeed. A remarkably similar idea of something superpowerful is found in Chinese culture – a tiger with wings.

 FOOD FOR THOUGHT

Was Grendel a real person? Probably not, but as a symbol of an enemy tribe he must have seemed a fearsome enemy. Many of these heraldic monsters are symbols of synergy, of the power gained through cooperation with others. They embody the challenge, 'You and whose army?', a clear threat to your enemies that if they cross you, they also cross your allies. The concept of mixed breeds still scares us. Just look at the horror story of The Fly in which a laboratory accident forces a man and a fly to become one fearsome creature. Modern-day horror tales of genetic mutation and experiments continue to inspire monstrous tales.

CHIMAERA

In Greek mythology, this fire-breathing monster had the body of a lion, a goat's head emerging from its back, and a serpent as its tail. A fearsome creature, its origin can be traced to the geography around the Chimaera volcano in Lycia, an ancient region on the coast of south west Asia Minor. It had a fiery summit, lions in its upper forests, goats on the lower slopes, and serpents in the marshes at its foot.

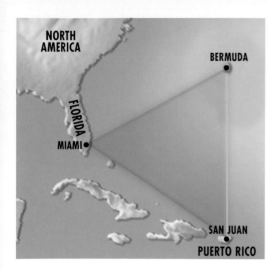

THE BERMUDA TRIANGLE

In 1945, five Avenger bomber planes took off from Fort Lauderdale in America and disappeared without trace near the Bermudas, a small group of islands in the Atlantic Ocean. The boat sent to search for them also vanished. Since then, hundreds of other ships and planes have disappeared in the same triangle of sea. Explanations have included alien abduction, sea monsters and unusual magnetic forces. A magnetic storm could have caused intruments to fail, or lost pilots may have run out of fuel.

FOOD FOR THOUGHT

The law of probability suggests that out of a huge number of predictions, some of them are bound to come true. Those that don't are quickly forgotten. The same law can be applied to the Bermuda Triangle. In any area of 647,500 square kilometres, disappearances are not uncommon, and the Bermuda Triangle is an area of extreme weather conditions. Probability could also be a factor in the curse of Tutankhamun – opening a tomb sealed for over 3,000 years could release unknown airborne bacteria. However, people have an appetite for myth and, today, the Internet spreads and embellishes modern myths far more quickly than has ever before been possible. If they are appealing and plausible enough they will spread, whether or not there is any real evidence to support them.

MYSTERY, MYTH & PROPHECY

It is human nature to endeavour to understand the nature of what happens around us. Until we understand unexplained events we cannot make informed choices about how to react to them. Myths usually start after something incredible has happened for which there seems no rational explanation. As science advances, more is understood about the world and how it works. Nevertheless, many mysteries endure. Strange events occur every day and, because it takes time to make sense of them, myths can sometimes grow to epic proportions. Mysteries, like our belief in psychic phenomena, are complex to unravel since they involve the nature of belief itself.

THE CURSE OF TUTANKHAMUN

In 1922, the tomb of the Pharaoh Tutankhamun (1336-1327 BCE) was discovered by Howard Carter, an archaeologist working for Lord Carnarvon. It is rumoured that Carter destroyed an inscription in the tomb which read: *Death will slay with his wings whoever disturbs the Pharaoh's peace.* A legacy of death did seem to follow the excavation. Lord Carnarvon died in 1923, aged 57. Then an archaeologist, an American financier, and a British industrialist all died after visiting the tomb. During the next seven years, 22 more people connected with the discovery also died; many in unusual circumstances. However, Carter himself lived another 17 years and died aged 65.

LOST BENEATH THE WAVES

The lost continent of Atlantis was said to have been the centre of a highly advanced civilization. According to ancient legends, Atlantean scientists under-stood the human mind and were great magicians. Atlantis was said to have been destroyed by a simultaneous volcanic eruption, earthquake and tidal wave, but some Atlanteans escaped and preserved their magical arts. No convincing geological or archaeological evidence has ever been found.

TITANIC DISASTER

Extraordinarily, some disasters are foretold. Predictions can be recorded before an event, which may seem to prove an ability to foretell the future. Before major disasters, such as the sinking of the *Titanic*, the calamity is often predicted, sometimes with detailed accounts of what will occur. One theory is that disasters involve so many deaths they create an energy which can be felt by sensitive psychics. This cannot be proven, although many people who do not consider themselves psychic also experience premonitions of danger.

NOSTRADAMUS AND PROPHECIES

Nostradamus was a French doctor known for his treatment of plague in the 16th century. In 1555, he published a book of obscure prophecies in the form of quatrains (poems in four lines). His followers believe he predicted various important events of later centuries, but his prophecies are so vague it is difficult to match them to specific incidents. This prophecy was interpreted as foretelling the 1945 bombing of Hiroshima and Nagasaki in Japan: *Near the harbour and in two cities will be two scourges, the like of which have never been seen. Hunger, plague within, people thrown out by the sword will cry for help from the great immortal God.*

ECTOPLASM

This medium is emitting ectoplasm. Ectoplasm is allegedly a substance called up out of the medium's body to give a spirit physical reality. Silvery-white in colour, it resembles thin fabric and forms the body and clothes of a spirit while it is communicating. Touching a spirit formed of ectoplasm is said to cause the medium to become ill. Although it hasn't been proved that all mediums fake the ectoplasm, it is possible to swallow a skein of cotton and gradually regurgitate it.

REST IN PEACE?

The words Rest in Peace carved on tombstones imply that the dead might not necessarily rest or be at peace. Over the centuries, many stories have evolved about ghosts who do not rest. They haunt people or places for revenge or because they have left something undone in their lives. Some people have reported that they live comfortably with supernatural neighbours. Others say ghosts are dangerous and can smash objects, make eerie noises, and create a perceptible aura of menace in a house.

CLAIRVOYANTS & MEDIUMS

Clairvoyancy is one of the earliest documented psychic phenomena and one of the most lucrative for hoaxers. Clairvoyants and mediums claim that, through them, we can contact the spirit of a dead person. Some mediums only claim to be able to speak with these spirits, others claim they can give them a physical form. Mediums have often been exposed as hoaxers or have admitted to defrauding their clients. A grieving person's fervent wish to contact a dead person they love makes them susceptible to such hoaxes. Although many mediums have undoubtedly claimed abilities they do not possess, clairvoyancy has yet to be fully investigated.

QUESTIONING THE SPIRITS

It may seem strange today, but in ancient times it was common to ask spirits for advice. Oracles were visionaries who went into a trance to ask questions on behalf of seekers. One of the most famous was Pythia, the Oracle at Delphi in Greece. She used volcanic fumes and drugs to assist her visions. Although ancient and modern mediums have posed many questions to the spirits and entered into long conversations with some of them, no real answers have ever been obtained about life after death or to prove the existence of spirits.

CONTACTING THE DEAD

To contact the spirits, mediums hold a seance. A group of people who wish to speak with a dead person, or perhaps ask about the afterlife, form a circle around a table and hold hands while the medium attempts to summon the presence of a spirit. Mediums have been known to fake the responses of spirits by using devices that strike the underside of the table to produce ghostly knocks in reply to questions. However, some mediums have produced inexplicable effects under test conditions designed by scientists attempting to expose them as frauds.

THE CASE OF KATIE KING

One famous medium was investigated by the Victorian scientist William Crookes. Florence Cook claimed she could manifest the spirit of Katie King (right) who appeared at seances and talked to guests. Florence was suspected of dressing up as the spirit herself or of having an accomplice do so. Crookes asserted that his investigation had convinced him of the spirit's existence. Crookes didn't publish his finding in any scientific journals but he never retracted his claims. Later, it was alleged that he had helped in the medium's fraud in order to have an affair with her.

 FOOD FOR THOUGHT

If there is life after death, then it would seem reasonable for dead spirits to want to contact the living. Ghosts might be trying to draw attention to the identity of their killer, or to where they buried the family silver. Spirits contacted by mediums might want their relatives to know they are happy and at peace. Some mediums are fakes who take advantage of people who are vulnerable after the death of someone they loved.
In their own defence, mediums might say they are only trying to provide comfort for the bereaved. And just because some are fakes it doesn't prove they all are. Some could be genuine.

SPIRITS & SPIRITUALISM

People who claim to possess psychic abilities often believe in the existence of spirits – non-physical beings who are thought to be gods or the souls of the dead. Some claim they can contact spirits using psychic powers. Spirits can be benevolent, guiding or teaching the humans they care about. But some malicious spirits are believed to return to the physical world to deliberately cause harm. Some spirits are tricksters; amused by the antics of mortals, they play jokes on people who attempt to contact them. Even among spiritualists and practitioners of magic who believe in the existence of spirits, there is no consistent theory about what they are or what methods should be used to communicate with them.

SPIRIT GUIDES

Shamans, like other kinds of magicians, use spirit guides as aids and symbols in their magic. Brazilian shamans believe people have spirits shaped like different animals, the most powerful of which is the jaguar. Native American shamanism involves attuning magic to the path of a different animal. A wolf shaman is expected to be tireless and fierce, while a coyote shaman is a devious trickster. Spirit guides are not necessarily animals. In shamanic magic, strong images and physical symbols are important. The greater the belief in a symbol, the greater its power.

REINCARNATION

Many people believe that after death our soul is reincarnated (reborn) in another body. Buddhists believe that good or evil deeds in one life will be rewarded or punished in the next. Hindus believe a human who leads an evil life may be reincarnated as an animal. Those who lead worthy lives attain ever-higher levels of enlightenment in each life until they pass on to the next stage of existence. Regression hypnotists have put people into a trance-like state in which they recall events apparently from their previous lives. Some people have even spoken in languages they do not know in their present life. However, it is difficult to prove or disprove the existence of reincarnation.

 FOOD FOR THOUGHT

Belief in the survival of the soul or spirit after death has been widespread throughout human history. It seems unbearable to think that we and the people we love will just stop existing when our body dies. And if we do have a spirit that exists independently of our body, why should other living things not have one as well?

BODY AND SOUL

The ancient Egyptians believed that in addition to the senses of the body, a person is divided into many different spiritual parts. Egyptian myths tell of great magicians who could separate their *ka* (soul or spirit double) from their body and fly in the form of a bird. Spells played an important part in the everyday lives of the Egyptians. They believed that all words have power and used them to bring about desired events or to curse their enemies.

DREAMTIME

Aboriginal Australians have a complex set of beliefs about the supernatural powers of their ancestors and the Dreamtime in which they created everything that now exists. As depicted in their rock paintings and artefacts, they see the natural world as a powerful and mysterious place with no distinction between the commonplace and the supernatural. They regard both as essential aspects of life.

SHAMANISM AND WITCH DOCTORS

Today, shamans like this one from Nigeria still watch over their peoples in Africa, South America, the Far East and the USA among its native Americans. A tribal shaman (witch doctor) is a magician and healer who cares for the body and soul of his people. He is as likely to be asked to hunt for a missing soul stolen by an enemy as a cure for illness. Shamanism is often passed on through families of witches. After their death, they are believed to continue as guardian spirits of their tribe.

MAGIC ENERGIES, PSYCHIC POWERS

Different belief systems have evolved around occult powers. Some beliefs involve worship and include psychic phenomena as aspects of religious activity. Some people believe paranormal powers are part of normal life and try to live according to complex rituals. Others fear any manifestation of the supernatural and try to ignore any evidence of or reference to it. Our fascination with the paranormal ensures that we will continue to investigate and attempt to understand supernatural abilities and events that do not conform to our existing ideas about the world.

CHAKRA POINTS

Chakra is the Hindu word to describe the main centres of spiritual power in the human body, points along the spine where energy is believed to be transformed into a usable form. Raw energy is said to be drawn from the Earth and fed into the chakra points. There are seven principle chakras in the body and detailed maps of the chakra and their connecting meridians and pathways have been used in Eastern mysticism and medicine for thousands of years.

LEGENDARY TREASURES

Similar to the balance of the elements (earth, fire, air and water) is the traditional pagan belief in four legendary items of great power. In mythology, these treasures are usually a sword, a spear, a cup, and a stone. Each has different powers and stories attached to it. Pagan legends tell of the Cauldron of Dagda, a cup of plenty said to provide a never-ending supply of food. The four objects are also symbols in the Tarot, a deck of cards used in fortune-telling. Magical items feature throughout history. During World War II Hitler collected such objects, believing they would make him invincible.

RITUAL PAINTINGS

The life of the Navaho Indians, a native American tribe who live by the border of Arizona and New Mexico, involves close attention to ritual and magical rites. The Navaho live in harmony with the environment and carry out their daily activities with customs and chants intended to bring good fortune and to ward off evil. One of their most impressive rituals is the curing ceremony, presided over by a medicine man (sorcerer who tends the spiritual well-being of a tribe). It involves drawing elaborate paintings in sand, which they believe helps to cure illness. Rather than magic, perhaps such rituals help to focus the mind. Believing they'll work may be enough to make them work.

CHI ENERGY

The Chinese discipline of *chi* is used in acupuncture healing and in the martial art, *t'ai chi ch'uan*. *Chi* is the energy that exists in all living things. This belief also exists in other cultures and religions. The yin-yang in Taoism symbolizes the two opposite and complementary forces of cosmic energy. Yin is feminine and negatively charged; yang is male and positively charged. Each contains part of the other, as seen in the yin-yang symbol at the centre of this picture of three *t'ai chi* sages. It is possible that a master of *chi* can imbue an object with more *chi*. Uncharacteristically, the Sony Corporation funded a seven-year project into psychic phenomena. These tests included a *chi* practitioner attempting to project *chi* energy into one of two glasses of water. A second *chi* practitioner then attempted to identify the glass with more *chi* energy. These tests are said to have had a 70 per cent success rate, but the test conditions and controls have not been verified.

FOOD FOR THOUGHT

Well-established magical systems, such as chi, can be as clearly thought out and consistent as conventional scientific knowledge. In China, for example, acupuncture (a treatment based on the chi system) has been accepted as scientifically valid for hundreds of years. It took a long time for Western doctors to take it seriously as a medical treatment. Other healing systems could offer the same.

BLOOD MAGIC

One belief common to different kinds of practising magicians concerns the power of blood. Black magic ceremonies, voodoo and African shamanism all include rites that involve sacrificing animals, usually a black cockerel or a goat although other animals may be used.

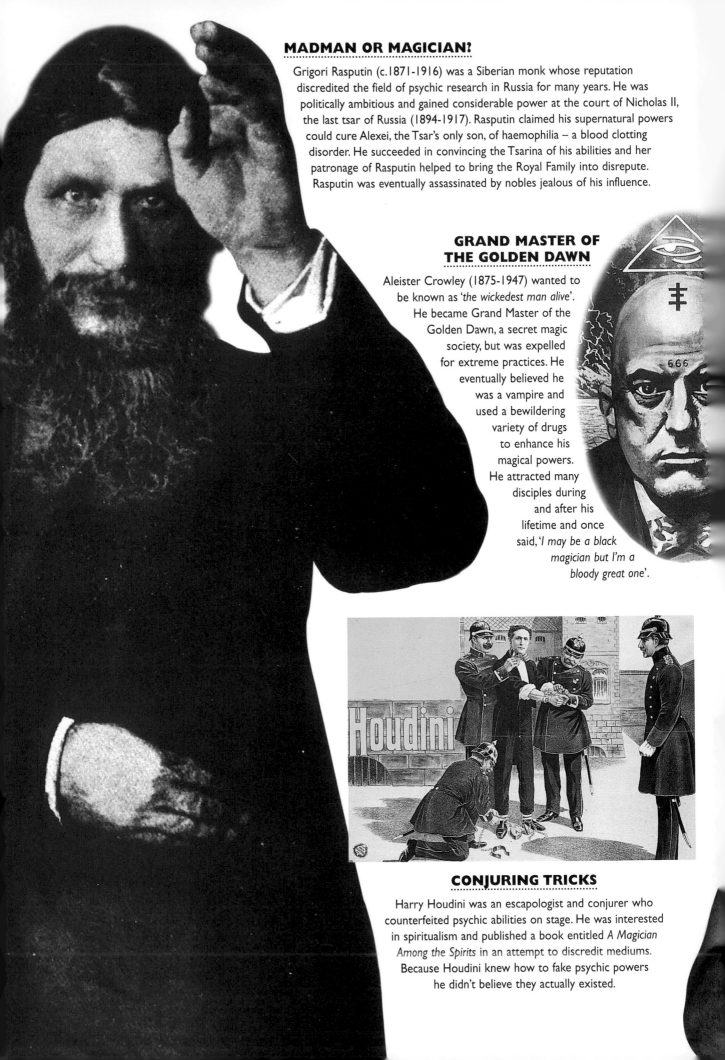

MADMAN OR MAGICIAN?

Grigori Rasputin (c.1871-1916) was a Siberian monk whose reputation discredited the field of psychic research in Russia for many years. He was politically ambitious and gained considerable power at the court of Nicholas II, the last tsar of Russia (1894-1917). Rasputin claimed his supernatural powers could cure Alexei, the Tsar's only son, of haemophilia – a blood clotting disorder. He succeeded in convincing the Tsarina of his abilities and her patronage of Rasputin helped to bring the Royal Family into disrepute. Rasputin was eventually assassinated by nobles jealous of his influence.

GRAND MASTER OF THE GOLDEN DAWN

Aleister Crowley (1875-1947) wanted to be known as 'the wickedest man alive'. He became Grand Master of the Golden Dawn, a secret magic society, but was expelled for extreme practices. He eventually believed he was a vampire and used a bewildering variety of drugs to enhance his magical powers. He attracted many disciples during and after his lifetime and once said, 'I may be a black magician but I'm a bloody great one'.

CONJURING TRICKS

Harry Houdini was an escapologist and conjurer who counterfeited psychic abilities on stage. He was interested in spiritualism and published a book entitled *A Magician Among the Spirits* in an attempt to discredit mediums. Because Houdini knew how to fake psychic powers he didn't believe they actually existed.

CONJURERS OR MAGICIANS?

Paranormal phenomena and psychic powers are often faked by conjurers who develop techniques to entertain or deceive their credulous audiences. Some stage magicians freely admit that their feats, such as mind-reading and levitation, are tricks; while others claim their abilities are genuine. Magicians such as Aleister Crowley and Grigori Rasputin managed to convince themselves and other people that their psychic talents were real. But their authenticity is doubted because of the money and sense of power that such magicians gain from their activities.

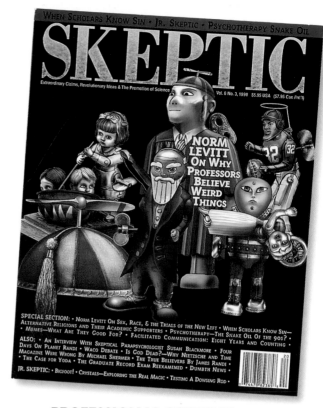

WHEN SCHOLARS KNOW SIN · JR. SKEPTIC · PSYCHOTHERAPY: SNAKE OIL

SKEPTIC

Extraordinary Claims, Revolutionary Ideas & The Promotion of Science

Vol. 6 No. 3, 1998 $5.95 USA ($7.95 Can /Int'l)

NORM LEVITT ON WHY PROFESSORS BELIEVE WEIRD THINGS

SPECIAL SECTION: · NORM LEVITT ON SEX, RACE, & THE TRIALS OF THE NEW LEFT · WHEN SCHOLARS KNOW SIN—ALTERNATIVE RELIGIONS AND THEIR ACADEMIC SUPPORTERS · PSYCHOTHERAPY—THE SNAKE OIL OF THE 90S? · MEMES—WHAT ARE THEY GOOD FOR? · FACILITATED COMMUNICATION: EIGHT YEARS AND COUNTING ·
ALSO: · AN INTERVIEW WITH SKEPTICAL PARAPSYCHOLOGIST SUSAN BLACKMORE · FOUR DAYS ON PLANET RANDI · WACO DEBATE · IS GOD DEAD?—WHY NIETZSCHE AND TIME MAGAZINE WERE WRONG BY MICHAEL SHERMER · THE TRUE BELIEVERS BY JAMES RANDI · THE CASE FOR YODA · THE GRADUATE RECORD EXAM REEXAMINED · DUMBTH NEWS ·
JR. SKEPTIC: · BIGFOOT! · CRYSTALS—EXPLORING THE REAL MAGIC · TESTING A DOWSING ROD ·

PROFESSIONAL SCEPTICS

A sceptic always doubts and questions accepted beliefs, mistrusts new theories and ideas until scientifically proven and even then tends to think nothing is certain. *Skeptic* magazine attempts to refute beliefs which in its opinion are '*180 degrees out of phase with reason*'.

THE POWER OF THE MIND

Uri Geller is a stage magician who claims to use the power of his mind to bend metal objects, restart watches and force computers to malfunction. He has performed these feats and others under strict test conditions but has also been exposed as a fake by people who claim to have seen him falsifying his demonstrations. Since Uri Geller was originally an amateur conjurer, people tend to doubt his psychic abilities. The phenomenon of metal-bending is not unique to Geller. It has been studied in others who claim to possess a similar power, as well as replicated by metallurgists (experts in metals and their properties).

FOOD FOR THOUGHT

It is impossible to prove that a conjurer does not have magical powers. It may be possible to reproduce the same results by non-magical means but that is not the same. Not many people really believe stage magicians have genuine magical powers, but it is more fun to suspend one's disbelief and enjoy the show. The ingenuity with which some conjuring tricks are devised – levitating, or making a railway carriage disappear – is often more impressive than if magic were actually being used.

MYSTICISM & MIRACLES

The psychic powers sometimes attributed to prophets and mystics may be believed in religious contexts but their existence has not been proven scientifically. Every major religion has accounts of miracles performed by priests and saints who possessed unusual and powerful abilities. Religious believers claim their god or gods bestow such powers on their followers in times of crisis. The evidence for the existence of miracles is difficult to trust because 'miraculous' events can be faked. However, the evidence is just as difficult to disprove because we understand so little about psychic phenomena.

THE TURIN SHROUD

First displayed in 1353 the Turin Shroud, which has the image of a crucified man imprinted on it, was said to be the burial sheet of Jesus Christ. In 1989, carbon-dating techniques were used to determine its age. Now generally accepted, the results dated the shroud between 1260 and 1390 – centuries later than Christ's crucifixion. However, there have been allegations that anti-clerical scientists faked the carbon-dating tests and the shroud is still venerated as a holy relic.

STIGMATA

A well-documented religious phenomenon, stigmata are the five wounds left on Christ after he was nailed to the cross. Since the crucifixion similar wounds have appeared spontaneously on certain people, such as Antonio Ruffini (right). They are generally passionate Christians but have nothing else in common. Stigmata do not seem to be caused by disease or self-inflicted injury. Some people's wounds last for years, others heal quickly. Today, stigmata remain a scientific mystery and are considered by the Roman Catholic Church to be a miracle.

HEALING POWERS

Certain religious statues and paintings are believed to have miraculous powers, capable of healing people of minor and even terminal illness. Every year, thousands of people make pilgrimages to religious sites and for many of them it is their last hope of becoming well. These 'cures' often have an immediate beneficial effect but it has yet to be proved that they make long-term improvements to health. One such statue said to possess the power to heal is the Madonna at Lourdes in France (left).

THE RESURRECTION OF CHRIST

Common to many religions, resurrection is one of the most impressive of alleged miracles. Sceptics who don't believe in divine miracles, or followers of different religious beliefs, sometimes claim that the prophets and demi-gods of ancient religions were people with powerful psychic powers.

FAKIRS

Indian fakirs enter a trance-like state in order to perform astounding feats of endurance. In 1835, the Maharaja of Lahore asked a fakir named Haridas to demonstrate his abilities. Haridas was buried underground in a padlocked coffin with barley sown in the earth above it. Forty days later Haridas was exhumed alive and well. He was never found to have cheated. Fakirs still give displays of their powers, which include lying unhurt on a bed of nails, walking on hot coals and levitation. Although these psychic phenomena have been well documented, scientists are still trying to work out how some of them are done.

BLACK HATS & BROOMSTICKS

Women believed to have magic power are called witches. According to folklore, witches wear black, ride a broomstick, brew magic potions in a cauldron, and have a familiar (spirit helper), often in the form of a cat. If any of this were true, witches would be very easy to identify. In the past, many women in England were persecuted for being witches just because they lived alone or used herbs to cure illnesses. The old superstitions inspired many fictional characters in fairy tales and other literature, such as Shakespeare's play, *Macbeth*.

DEADLY NIGHTSHADE

When consumed or smoked, some plants have properties that cause people to have fearful visions or strange sensations.

Belladonna (deadly nightshade), a poisonous herb, was often used in magical rites. It can cause the hallucination of flying, which may be why some people believed they were witches and confessed to having flown by magical means.

FOOD FOR THOUGHT

The author Arthur C. Clarke wrote: 'Any sufficiently advanced technology is indistinguishable from magic.' Many of the things we take for granted – radio, computers, and aeroplanes – would have seemed magical to our ancestors.

It is human nature to look for explanations for what we do not understand, and 'magic' can be used to explain almost anything! It may be that there are new sciences, not currently known to us, which could explain some of these phenomena. And perhaps the idea of magic is more attractive to us because we have no explanation for it.

THE COURT MAGICIAN

An English scholar, Dr John Dee (1527-1608) was a mathematician and astrologer who studied sorcery and practised as a magician at various European courts. He claimed angels had taught him magic spells and *Enoch*, the language which Adam supposedly spoke in the Garden of Eden. Queen Elizabeth I chose January 14 for her coronation because Dr Dee told her that date was astrologically fortunate. A black obsidian mirror, which he said had been given to him by an angel, can still be seen at the British Museum.

WITCHES & WARLOCKS

W hen events and our sense of things seem beyond understanding, humankind has tended to attribute them to the existence of psychic abilities or supernatural powers. Such beliefs are often found underlying religions, superstitions, and mysteries. All through the 20th century, scientists have sought explanations for a variety of psychic phenomena, but there remains much to discover and to understand. To unravel their mysteries and evaluate the evidence we must first explore the history of beliefs in the paranormal.

MAGIC OF THE GODS

The priests and priestesses of ancient religions used magical rites in their ceremonies. Gods such as the Egyptian Isis (above) and the Persian Mithras had mysteries into which only their followers were initiated. Becoming one with the god was the main aspiration. Isis was a goddess of love, death, cunning, and magic. Hieroglyphs and magical inscriptions adorned her temples. Because Isis means wisdom, her supporters were expected to be intelligent and reasoning. Plutarch, an ancient Greek philosopher, described Isis worshippers as seekers of the hidden truths behind the gods.

A DEMONIC PACT

Witches and warlocks were suspected of being in league with the Devil, who gave them magical powers in return for their souls. Anyone who claimed they could do magic was therefore believed to be unholy. The English dramatist Christopher Marlowe (1564-93) and the German poet Johann Wolfgang von Goethe (1749-1832) both wrote plays about Georg Faust (1480-1538), a legendary German magician who sold his soul in return for increased knowledge. From within the protection of a ritual circle, Dr Faust is shown here summoning Mephistopheles, an agent of the Devil.

73

WARDS AGAINST EVIL

Many customs and superstitions are based on magic. Most of them are designed to ward off evil influences but they also often ascribe magic powers to certain items. For example a horseshoe hung over a doorway is thought to prevent witches from entering.

BLACK & WHITE MAGIC

Magic practices traditionally fall into one of two categories. Black magic includes magic rites that make use of blood, death and the name of the Devil. White magic encompasses powers of healing, visions and some religious ceremonies. Some people practise magic today but, in most cases, without the rituals and formulae used in past. Not all practitioners of magic think of themselves as either black or white magicians. Some consider the study of magic to be a science which can be used for either good or evil purposes. Others deliberately choose to study only white or black magic.

 FOOD FOR THOUGHT

Witchcraft used to be a convenient excuse for misfortune. If a cow fell sick or a field was blighted, it was easier to blame an old woman who lived alone, rather than to accept that you had been unlucky, or even that you had not looked after it properly. Fear of witchcraft spread quickly, and anyone who did not join in the condemnation of witches, might have been accused of being one. This led to massive witch trials such as those in Salem, Massachusetts in 1692, when more than 150 people from one village were arrested in anti-witchcraft hysteria. In 17th-century Europe, even a birthmark could brand you as a witch, and 40,000 people were executed in Britain alone – a small fraction of the total in Europe as a whole.

CRYSTAL HEALING

It is a long-held belief that crystals and semi-precious stones have magic healing properties. In Egypt, magicians sometimes advised people to eat the powdered remains of magical amulets to cure illness. This belief is still popular today, with crystal healers claiming they can cure minor illnesses. Some even say that crystals are effective against more dangerous diseases. A crystal is simply placed against the skin of a patient but sometimes it is still powdered and ingested.

DEVIL WORSHIP

Witches and black magicians who made pacts with the Devil held ceremonies to worship him. The Black Mass was a corruption of Christian worship designed to summon the Devil and typically involved acts of deliberate evil designed to please him. The Witches' Sabbat was a midnight ritual in which witches and demons danced around a fire. The tradition is probably connected to older Celtic festivals held on May Eve and Hallowe'en. Although the Witches' Sabbat is still held today, it is not necessarily with the intent to summon the Devil. It can also be held as a celebration of birth and new life.

SOLOMON THE MAGICIAN

In the 10th century, King Solomon of Israel was said to be a great magician. The *Key of Solomon*, one of the oldest known books of spells, tells how he '*discovered the secret of how to shut a million satanic spirits in a bottle of black glass, together with seventy-two of their kings*'. The book was used by black magicians because it also told how to make a pact with the Devil, summon spirits, gain fortunes, and extend life. Solomon's Seal (two interlocked triangles) is often used in magic rites.

VOODOO

Voodoo is a religious cult practised in parts of Africa, South America and the Caribbean. It evolved as a combination of Catholicism and West African tradition on 17th-century slave plantations. Voodoo followers believe that while in a trance, a person can be beneficially possessed by their ancestors or gods. However, it also has a dark side when used in black magic. Voodoo sorcerers claim they can create zombies – people raised from the dead who are subject to the will of the sorcerer and obey his commands. Voodoo dolls are made by sorcerers using hair or nail clippings of a living individual. Sticking pins into the doll is believed to harm the person it represents.

BOARD GAMES

Originally called the planchette, Ouija dates from the 1850s and was a triangular board supported by two wheels and a pencil. The pressure of hands placed on the surface moved the board and the pencil wrote messages (apparently from the spirits) on a piece of paper beneath it. In 1868, American toy companies copied and refined the idea to include the letters of the alphabet and the words 'yes' and 'no'. The planchette then only had to move from letter to letter to spell out its message. A Ouija board is a popular way of contacting spirits during a seance, although the messages can easily be faked by players controlling the planchette.

RECEPTIVE MINDS

Meditation is a technique of clearing the mind. Many psychic practitioners use it to prepare their mind to be receptive to telepathic thoughts, or messages from the spirit world. Meditation is also used in prayer, in healing and as a relaxation technique. Prolonged meditation induces a trance-like state in which all the capabilities of the mind are concentrated on a single thought. Yoga is an Asian meditative technique that has become increasingly popular in the West.

MUSIC FROM THE GRAVE

Some mediums specialize in contacting the spirits of celebrities. Rosemary Brown, a London housewife, claims she has been contacted by the spirits of many eminent composers such as Beethoven who dictated musical scores to her. Experts have said her work is more than just imitation but Rosemary's lack of musical training means she has only been able to retrieve fragments. Another medium, Stella Horrocks, produces whole novels which she claims have been dictated to her by dead authors such as Jane Austen. She goes into a trance to write and the handwriting for each novelist is different.

EXORCISM

Some branches of the Christian Church still perform exorcisms. These rituals are intended not to summon spirits but to dispel them. In the Bible, exorcisms are performed to cast out demons who have possessed a person's body. Nowadays, exorcism is used to dispel ghosts or spirits. An exorcist commands the possessing spirit to depart using the name of God to enforce his injunction. Exorcism, like a powerful spell, requires three items for the ritual – a bible, a bell, and a candle.

CHANNELLING THE SUPERNATURAL

Many psychics and mediums believe the spirit world can be channelled and used to put people in touch with their own unconscious minds. Some psychics believe people leave images of themselves wherever they have been. Police have occasionally hired psychics to help catch criminals, identifying them by the psychic impression left at a crime scene. Psychics have also been known to track down missing people, both alive and dead. Many techniques are used to contact supernatural entities, including hypnotism and drugs, which can be highly dangerous. This sheer variety of methods is one reason why scientists have found it difficult to formulate theories about the alleged paranormal abilities of psychics and mediums.

AUTOMATIC WRITING

Writing without conscious control could be thought of as receiving messages from the spirit world. The subject enters a trance while holding a writing implement and watching the reflection of a candle in a mirror. The writing produced is usually disjointed and incomprehensible but is sometimes treated as if full of meaning. This is not generally regarded as a very credible spiritualist technique because the trance state can easily be faked.

 ## FOOD FOR THOUGHT

Channelling methods assume that spirits can be controlled or contacted by living people through the power of rituals. Whether they are trying to banish a spirit or asking it for help, people use special items, words, music, mental preparation, or some combination of these, to open up a link between themselves and the spirit. The ritual may be intended to affect the spirit, strengthening or weakening its hold on the ordinary world. Or it may be intended to affect the person who is conducting it, raising their own spirit to a 'higher plane'. It's easier to judge whether something has worked on yourself than on another spirit.

TERMS USED IN DIVINATION

Astrology
Divination using the signs of the zodiac.

Cartomancy
Fortune-telling with playing cards.

Catoptromancy
Using mirrors to divine the future.

Chiromancy
Reading the lines on a person's hand to see their future, and character.

Geomancy
Telling the future through observation of land forms or the patterns made by dust on a flat surface.

Metascopy
Telling fortunes from lines on the forehead.

Necromancy
Gaining information from the dead.

Oneiromancy
Telling the future from dreams.

Rhabdomancy
Dowsing to find water, treasure or lost objects.

CROSS MY PALM WITH SILVER

Commercial divination has been around for centuries but is most often perceived as connected to the Romany or gypsy lifestyle. Traditionally, Romany blood bestows strong psychic powers on those who inherit it. Gypsies, who used to travel widely across Europe in caravans, were seen as accomplished fortune-tellers. A crystal ball is often used by fortune-tellers and mediums who claim they can divine the future by looking into its depths.

DIVINATION

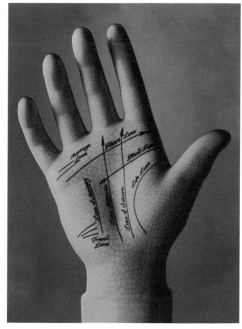

Divination means to foretell the future or, by magical, mystical or supernatural means, to reveal what is hidden. Many of the divining methods that have been used for centuries are still in use today. Divination often involves a predefined set of symbols which can represent emotions, events, and personal qualities. By selecting these symbols, seemingly at random, and observing which ones occur in a particular pattern, fortune-tellers make predictions about the future. Other forms of divination involve seeing visions of the future or making observations based on the physical qualities of an individual.

PALM READING

Palmistry, or chiromancy, is a form of divination which involves interpreting the lines on the palm of a hand. Unlike Tarot, Rune-casting, and *I Ching*, chiromantic predictions are based on an observed quality of the individual. Palmists associate each line on the hand with a different aspect of life. These definitions have developed gradually but are generally held to include: the Life Line, the Health Line, the Line of Fortune and the Line of Fate. Breaks and bends in the various lines signify important events in a person's life.

THE ZODIAC

The Ram, the Bull, the Heavenly Twins.
Next to the Crab, the Lion shines, the Virgin and the Scales.
The Scorpion, Archer and He-Goat,
The Man who carries the Watering Pot and the
Fish with the glittering tails.

This verse, *The Hunt of the Heavenly Host*, helps us to remember the 12 astrological symbols which make up the Zodiac, a system used in several divining techniques. The position of the planets, Sun, Moon, and signs of the zodiac at the time of a person's birth is believed to define their nature. The signs are divided into four groups associated with the elements: earth, fire, air and water. For example, Leo, a fire sign is associated with adventure and ambition.

FOOD FOR THOUGHT

Divination or guesswork? Accomplished fortune-tellers can make educated guesses about the future of a client simply by assessing their appearance and personality. Predicting romance for a pretty girl or good fortune for someone who looks prosperous is almost certain to be accurate.

CASTING THE ORACLE

Divination often involves throwing down small objects and reading the pattern they make. Ancient practitioners described this method of divination as casting the oracle. Originally, these methods were used for practical purposes rather than as entertainment and the objects used were simple things that were easily found or made. Over the years, rituals developed around the various forms of divination and the sets of cards, stones, and sticks used became increasingly elaborate and ornamental.

FORTUNE-TELLING WITH TEA LEAVES

Reading fortunes in the tea leaves is not much in favour now that tea usually comes packaged in teabags. Reading the tea leaves is a simple form of divination. Once the tea in a cup has been drunk, the cup is turned anti-clockwise three times. The patterns the leaves form are read to predict coming events. Romany gypsies have a whole symbolic language with which to interpret the images. A padlock, for example, indicates a door to success is about to open.

RUNE STONES

Casting rune stones is an ancient Scandinavian form of divination. The word *runa* means mystery in Anglo-Saxon. Rune Masters were tribal magicians who used the power of their hidden language to affect the weather, the harvest, healing, war, and love.

The traditional Germanic set of runes uses an alphabet of three sets of eight runes beginning with the *futhark*. Later alphabets contain a blank rune to represent the unknowable. As with cards used in divination, the runes are drawn unseen and laid down in a pattern which allows their symbolic meanings to be applied to a particular question.

DOWSING FOR WATER

Dowsing is simply water-divining, although some dowsers can also trace electrical cables, minerals, and oil. To the extent that it is no longer regarded as especially paranormal, dowsing has become accepted in the modern world. Traditionally, a forked stick is held out by a dowser as he or she walks through the countryside. If water is nearby, usually under the earth, the dowsing rod twitches. It has been suggested that dowsers are particularly sensitive to the Earth's magnetic field. However, some dowsers have found water by holding a pendulum over a map.

THE MAGICIAN.

I

ⴲ The Magician ☿

THE TAROT

The Tarot is a special deck of cards used for divination. Instead of the four suits of hearts, spades, diamonds and clubs of a deck of playing cards, the Tarot deck uses suits of cups, swords, wands and discs. Each suit has an additional court card. The Tarot deck also contains 22 greater trumps known as the Major Arcana. All the cards have symbolic associations as well as their apparent meaning. The different Tarot decks offer different interpretations. The Magician, for example, could mean willpower or skill. During a Tarot reading the cards are laid face down in certain positions to focus on different aspects of the subject's life. They are then turned over and interpreted.

THE I CHING

One of the oldest oracle books in the world, the Chinese *I Ching* or *Book of Changes* has lasted in its present form for at least 3000 years. Divination based on the *I Ching* does not predict specific events. Instead, it shows possible outcomes of certain actions. It is composed of 64 hexagrams in different combinations of six broken or unbroken lines. Using random activities such as drawing straws from a bundle or flipping a coin, a hexagram is produced and interpreted using the *I Ching*.

🗏 FOOD FOR THOUGHT

Some divination methods, such as cartomancy or tea-leaf reading, involve interpretation of random effects. Others study a quality of the person seeking information (the 'querent'), as in palmistry or astrology. The difference between them is an important one. It is easier to believe that the querent's character might express itself through the lines on their palm, or might be influenced by the time of year of their birth, than that their presence can affect the fall of cards or twigs. It is also possible that the random methods of divination are used to give the diviner time to assess a person's character and to formulate an appropriate prediction.

DREAMS & VISIONS

KUBLA KHAN'S PLEASURE DOME

In 1797, the poet Samuel Taylor Coleridge composed 300 lines of poetry while in an opium-induced sleep. When he woke he could remember the poem and began to write it down but after being interrupted by a visitor he was unable to recall the rest of the poem. There are many instances of other writers, musicians, and artists gaining inspiration from their dreams. Parapsychologists have speculated that the sense of PSI (paranormal sensory information) is not as strong as the senses of touch, taste, smell, hearing, and sight. Being weaker, it functions better when there are no distractions, such as while a person sleeps.

Scientists are still investigating the processes of the unconscious mind. In his analysis of how the unconscious works, the forerunner of modern psychology, Sigmund Freud (1856-1939) paid special attention to the role of dreams. A Swiss psychologist, Carl Jung (1875-1961), later proposed that everyone shared a collective unconscious in which certain archetypal images recur, each with its own symbolism. Until the 20th century, there was no concerted study of the human psyche. Psychology (study of the mind), like neuroscience (study of the brain), is still a young science. Parapsychology (study of psychic phenomena) draws on these other sciences but there is still much to be discovered.

REM SLEEP

The mind is active and people dream during the rapid eye movement (REM) stages of deep sleep. The body goes through five stages from deep to light sleep. During deep sleep, the body repairs itself. People dream every time they sleep although they might not remember their dreams. A technique known as lucid dreaming trains the sleeping mind to control the progress of dreams.

SLEEP RESEARCH

Studies conducted on sleeping people indicated they were more susceptible to receiving psychic messages while in their REM period of sleep. Experiments involved a psychic transmitting images to a sleeping psychic at different stages of a sleep cycle. Woken after each stage, the person could recall the images more successfully after REM sleep.

ANALYSIS OF DREAMS

There have been many theories about dreams. Ancient peoples believed they were messages from the gods. Freud, one of the first scientists who tried to explain dreaming, thought dreams were the wishes of the unconscious mind. More recently, Jung (right) wrote that in dreams, people harness their creativity and come to terms with their fears. Modern sleep research tends to indicate that dreams are the result of the firing of neurons in the brain to help in the process of storing memories. Dreams are closely linked with the study of psychic phenomena because both are workings of the mind which is only partly understood.

OUT-OF-BODY EXPERIENCES

Many people have reported having near-death or out-of-body experiences, and commonly describe this as seeing a bright light pulling the soul away from the body. When the person is revived they often report having watched their own unconscious body being brought back to life. This 'astral' body is claimed to be identical to the physical body but is transparent and shining. Ancient writings describe this phenomenon as a supernatural power that can be gained through magic or meditation. Sceptics prefer to put it down to hallucination or delusion.

 FOOD FOR THOUGHT

All of these dream and vision phenomena can be attributed to the mind behaving oddly when it is on the edge of consciousness or beyond. Surrealist artists such as Salvador Dalí deliberately induced this state in themselves. They believed it put them in touch with a higher level of reality and produced images intended to speak directly to their unconscious; perhaps drawing on universal symbols of a collective unconscious. Most people probably think they dream complex, strange and interesting stories that would make wonderful films or books. Dreams are never easy to write down when you've woken up, though!

EXPERIMENTS OF THE MIND

Parapsychology is the study of extraordinary mental phenomena, such as telepathy, that are experienced by human beings yet seem to have no physical cause. Many scientists are suspicious of parapsychology because it has become associated, wrongly, with other paranormal events such as alien abductions. Parapsychology research includes investigating extrasensory perception (ESP) which is the ability to receive information not available to the accepted five senses; psychokinesis (PK) which is the ability to alter the state of physical objects by mental activity alone; and out-of-body experiences. The study of parapsychology assumes that the potential of the human mind has been underestimated.

TELEPATHY

Paranormal research has recorded many instances of telepathy occurring in everyday life. Close family relationships, especially between twins, tend to increase the likelihood of telepathic connection. Some experiments in which the participants try to communicate over long distances have achieved impressive results. However, if ESP is some kind of mental radio, it is proving very difficult to tune. Despite the high success rates, experiments have yet to prove the existence of viable telepathic communication.

PHOTOGRAPHING AURAS

Many mediums have claimed they can see an aura of light around the human body. In 1939, a Russian engineer, Semyon Kirlian developed a diagnostic technique that could sense heat and electro-magnetic fields. He photographed these auras using an electric coil, an aluminium plate and photosensitive film covered by glass. His pictures showed people surrounded by a coloured halo of light.

MILITARY APPLICATIONS OF PSI

Ever since the days when magic was used to protect the tribe, psychic phenomena have been investigated as a potential military aid. During the Cold War (following World War II), the American and Russian governments conducted serious studies of paranormal sensory information (PSI) and how it could be used. For some years, a secret American Defense project at the Pentagon, known as operation Stargate, has been rumoured to be training psychics to use their abilities to see into enemy bases and to attempt to cause mental confusion in foreign military leaders.

JOSEPH RHINE

In 1927, Dr Joseph Rhine and his wife, Louisa, started the first investigation into ESP at Duke University in North Carolina. This was the beginning of the science of parapsychology. Rhine invented the term ESP and spent 50 years researching the phenomenon. His work was first published in 1934. Scientists immediately found fault with his laboratory techniques and statistical analysis. Rhine successfully defended his techniques, but many thought his studies must have been experimental fraud.

ZENER CARDS

One of the earliest experiments in detecting psychic ability were Zener cards, a deck of 25 cards divided into five sets of five cards, each with one of five different symbols on it. The cards were shuffled and, one at a time, a 'sender' would try to telepathically project the symbol on each card to someone across the room. That person would attempt to 'see' what card the sender was projecting. Rhine achieved a high success rate with this experiment under laboratory conditions. Some subjects were able to name the entire deck of cards correctly and others could predict in advance what order cards would be shuffled into.

MESMERIZING MINDS

Franz Mesmer (1734-1815) was an Austrian physician. He believed the human body has magnetic properties that could be used to cure illness. Mesmer undertook public healings which involved connecting people by cords to a tub of water filled with iron filings. He achieved some notable successes but the scientific community remained unconvinced and he was denounced as an impostor. Although Mesmer's work was largely discredited, it paved the way for the study of hypnotism and the unconscious mind.

KIRLIAN PHOTOGRAPHY

Some people who study paranormal events think that many of the so-called supernatural powers are natural to us. These may include the use of electrical and other energy fields. Semyon Kirlian's (see page 84) device could photograph the electrical and biogenetic energies transmitted by the human body. Although its use remains controversial, some doctors now use the technique to diagnose some cancers and psychological disorders. After death, a person's energies could perhaps leave behind a ghostly image.

A SHADOW OF OURSELVES

Another popular theory is that ghosts are human auras somehow trapped on this Earthly plane long after the people have died. Apparently, each of us radiates an invisible electro-magnetic energy field which in the past only people such as clairvoyants were able to detect. Modern science has confirmed that the human body emanates a field of energy that could be what has been described as an aura.

THE LITTLE PEOPLE

Folklore is full of tales of mythical creatures such as fairies, elves, and dwarves. Although these 'little people' are seen as purely fictional nowadays, it is possible that their origins could be traced to distant memories of creatures who did actually exist alongside man. Perhaps they still do and remain mostly elusive, but when they are seen we interpret their presence as ghostly.

BEINGS FROM OTHER WORLDS

There are many similarities between the reported sightings of ghosts and those of aliens coming to Earth in unidentified flying objects (UFOs). Both are elusive, visible only at certain times and by particular people. Perhaps they are different aspects of the same phenomenon. 'Aliens' may be manifestations of human spirits from Earth rather than from outer space.

PARALLEL WORLDS

Ghosts may not be the spirits of dead people from this world but are perhaps beings from a parallel world. They are not normally visible to our human senses but occasionally, when conditions are right, we may catch a glimpse of them. The idea of other worlds existing undetected alongside our own is a very old one. Some people like to think the creatures of folklore and mythology are not simply the product of human imagination but recalled memories of a time past when there was contact between our worlds. Parallels can be drawn to the animal kingdom in which creatures with a different range of senses to our own see an entirely different world to us, even though we occupy the same space and time on Earth.

TIME TRAVEL

For centuries, mankind has been fascinated by the idea of the past, present and future co-existing in parallel worlds, normally invisible to one another. Authors, such as H.G. Wells (1866-1946), and filmmakers have often used the idea. Although a controversial issue, the physicist Albert Einstein (1879-1955) used his theory of relativity to prove that the existence of parallel time and space is possible. If it is, then sightings of ghosts may be glimpses of people's past or future lives in another dimension.

CIRCLE OF HANDS

A long-established method of getting in touch with the spirit world is to conduct a seance. A group of people sit round a table in a quiet, darkened room. A medium, someone who is sensitive to the spirit world, acts as a go-between. Rituals are performed until the medium makes contact with a spirit and receives a message on behalf of one of the participants.

 FOOD FOR THOUGHT

Various forms of telepathy may be possible between some people, especially if they are closely related. They may be able to communicate thoughts without actually speaking. Perhaps mediums can pick up thoughts and feelings about a dead friend or relative from participants at a seance. If so, they would of course be accurate. However, mediums may just be excellent judges of character who, over the years, have become expert at telling people what they want to hear.

MENTAL RADIO

Recent paranormal research has been attempting to understand what happens when successful telepathic communication takes place. It may be possible to observe brain activity during a psychic episode by recording the pattern of brain-waves of an experimental subject. Some studies indicate there may be changes in alpha waves; the essential carrier signal for the operation of the mind, when psychic abilities are being used.

FOOD FOR THOUGHT

If ESP and telepathy can be shown to exist and people trained to use these abilities, there are endless practical uses for them. How great might be the impact on society if people could read each other's minds or communicate by thought alone? It might lead to a utopian future in which we live in blissful harmony; or perhaps a nightmarish spy-state in which none of our thoughts could be private. Many independent researchers agree that mental powers can affect mechanical systems. They now ask not 'Does it exist?' but 'What is it?'

BIOGENETIC FORCE

In 1926, Russia was one of the first countries to do scientific research into psychic phenomena. Soviet scientists investigated the physical conditions necessary to enable the mind to transmit energy. In the 1970s, they did extensive studies of a Russian housewife called Nina Kulagina. Under controlled laboratory conditions, she was able to move objects, create burn marks, and increase the magnetic properties of objects without any physical contact with them. The force Kulagina apparently possessed has been called bioenergetics.

ESP & PK

The two most widely researched areas of psychic phenomena are extrasensory perception (ESP) and psychokinesis (PK). ESP is generally held to include telepathy (direct mind to mind communication), precognition (having knowledge of unplanned future events), and clairvoyance (having second sight, or the ability to foretell future events). PK is the movement of objects by the power of thought alone. PK may explain the apparent existence of poltergeists, ghosts who cause apparently untouched objects to break or levitate. It has been suggested that a teenager in a highly charged mental response to emotional problems could cause spontaneous PK.

GANZFELD EXPERIMENTS

The ganzfeld (total field) experiment was designed by parapsychologists to counter claims of experimental error. To achieve a relaxed and receptive state, subjects were put into an environment free of all sensory influences from sight, sound, and touch. A sender then attempted to telepathically communicate a randomly-selected image to the receptive person. The receiver reported aloud all their thoughts, images, feelings, and impulses. The ganzfeld experiment achieved a high success rate. More subjects successfully projected and received images than would be predicted by the theory of probability.

RANDOM NUMBERS – DEFINITE RESULTS

Since electronic and computer technology became widespread, parapsychologists have conducted a series of experiments on the relationships between mind, matter, and energy. One such experiment measured the human ability to influence a random element, such as which number will be cast when a die is thrown. Random number generator (RNG) machines produce an electrical datastream that a test subject cannot modify by any physical means. Experiments established statistically that most humans *can* influence which numbers will come up randomly. The success rate seems higher at full moon; a time when magnetism in the brain may be affected by the Earth's magnetic field.

PSYCHOKINESIS

In the 1920s, Baron Albert von Schrenk-Notzing, an investigator of the paranormal, worked with Stanislava Tomczyk (right) and Willy Schneider to convince scientific observers and members of the English Society for Psychical Research that it was possible to levitate objects by no known physical means. Neither psychics nor Schrenk-Notzing were ever suspected of fraud.

ANCIENT UFOS

ALIEN FOOTPRINT

This fossilized hominid footprint from east Africa was made by an ordinary biped, yet the rock is 3.5 million years old! Some UFOlogists claim the print pre-dates *homo erectus* (prehistoric man) and that it was made by a visiting spaceman.

'**I**n the 30th year, in the 4th month, on the 5th day, by the river Chebar,' wrote the prophet Ezekiel in the Bible, 'I saw something that looked like burning coals of fire.' Ezekiel described how he saw wheels gleaming like a jewel, 'being as it were a wheel within a wheel'. This could be a description of a gyroscope. Ezekiel interpreted his experience as a vision of God. Nowadays, UFOlogists would suggest it was one of the first recorded sightings of an unidentified flying object (UFO).

ANCIENT ABDUCTIONS

Celtic legends told of faery beings who stole babies from their cots and replaced them with faery infants. To keep their babies safe, medieval peasants hung a knife over the cradle. Were these 'faeries' alien scientists?

FOOD FOR THOUGHT

'OCCAM'S RAZOR!'

The medieval thinker William Occam made famous a principle which, in today's language, amounts to: 'Don't invent new weird theories when a simple, common sense answer already exists.' Most of the evidence on this page has a perfectly reasonable explanation, without postulating visits by spacemen.

PREHISTORIC RECORDS

These prehistoric rock drawings from Peru seem to include astronauts wearing space helmets. Cave paintings sometimes show discs in the sky, and the Bible tells us that in prehistory 'the sons of God' came down and took human wives. Could these be ancient references to visits by spacemen?

A DESERT MYSTERY

Over 1,000 years ago, in Nazca, Peru, thousands of stones were arranged to make vast lines and huge figures in the desert. The images, including these 'aliens', are clearly visible from the air but are difficult to distinguish while standing beside them. In 1969, the writer Erich von Däniken suggested that 'ancient astronauts' interfered with humankind's technology and genes and thus shaped human history. He claimed that these Nazca lines were made to be seen by alien visitors from their spaceships.

CULTURAL TRACKING

A Bible story tells of the prophet Elijah being carried away by a chariot of fire. In 1897, Americans saw airships, but in the 1950s metal spaceships were seen (see pages 92-3). UFOs seem to appear in whatever form people expect to see them. This may account for the wide diversity of reported sightings.

c. 1450 BCE, EGYPT

Pharaoh Thutmose III sees 'circles of fire' in the sky.

322 BCE, LEBANON

Shining silver shields fly over a city besieged by Alexander the Great. They destroy the walls by firing beams of light at the defences.

840 CE, FRANCE

The Archbishop of Lyon stops people killing two creatures who had come to Earth in a 'cloud ship'.

1211, IRELAND

The people of Cloera try to catch creatures whose 'airship' had caught on their church roof.

1271, JAPAN

The execution of a Buddhist monk is called off when a bright object hangs in the sky above the site.

1492

A sailor on Columbus's ship, the Santa Maria, sees a glittering thing in the sky.

1639, BOSTON, USA

Mr James Everell and friends are fishing when a bright light hovers over them and moves their boat upstream.

1752, SWEDEN

Farmers see a large, shining cylinder in the sky 'give birth' to smaller balls of light.

1762, SWITZERLAND

In different towns, two astronomers independently record a 'spindle-shaped' aircraft move across the face of the Sun.

1819, MASSACHUSETTS, USA

Professor Rufus Graves sees a fireball crash into the yard of his friend Erastus Dewey. They find wreckage and, inside it, a foul-smelling pulpy substance.

1820, USA

Mormon leader Joseph Smith sees a UFO and talks with its occupants.

1861, CHILE

Peasants see a metal bird with shining eyes and scraping scales.

1868, ENGLAND

Astronomers at the Radcliffe Observatory, Oxford University, track a UFO for four minutes.

1887, BANJOS, SPAIN

Villagers found two 'children' in a cave. Their clothes were strange, they spoke no known language and their skin was green.

SIGHTINGS

UFOs undoubtedly exist. What is in doubt is what they are. Every year, over a thousand sightings are reported, many from people who ask to remain anonymous lest they be thought mad. Famous people who have seen **UFOs** include two American presidents; Jimmy Carter once watched a **UFO** while he was attending a dinner party; and President Reagan stunned a White House meeting by announcing he had once seen a **UFO** from the window of his plane. American astronaut Major Gordon Cooper reported seeing a glowing green object on his space flight in 1963 – an object that had also appeared on Australian radar. In 1965, space-walkers Ed White and James McDivitt reported seeing a metallic **UFO**, with 'arms' sticking out in all directions.

 FOOD FOR THOUGHT

In the 1960s, the American Air Force project Blue Book studied 13,000 UFO sightings. It found only about two per cent were really unidentified. Most UFOs are perfectly natural phenomena. Explanations include:
- *Aircraft and satellites.*
- *Weather balloons.*
- *Jupiter (and other planets) - often unusually bright. A visual illusion called autokinesis can make them seem to move in the sky.*
- *Meteors.*
- *Canadian scientists have found a correlation between UFO phenomena and earthquakes. Stress on rocks just before an earthquake can produce strong electrical fields and strange lights.*
- *Vitreous floaters (matter moving inside the eye itself).*
- *Wishful thinking, hysteria, and emotional disturbance.*

Yes, it is less romantic! But even the UFO sightings not yet explained are also likely to be attributable either to natural phenomena that we don't yet fully understand (such as ball lightning) or to military experiments.

ALIEN WARFARE

This woodcut from 1561 records a frightening event in Germany when black and red balls of light seemed to battle together in the sky. Some UFOlogists suggest that perhaps two alien species were fighting for control of the Earth.

A UFO OF THE NINETIES

Jeremy Johnson, who took this photograph in England in 1992, thought at first he had missed his chance, because the round white object vanished as soon as he pointed the camera at it.

THE AIRSHIP PHENOMENON

In 1897, many people in America saw shining, cigar-shaped 'airships'. This illustration was drawn for a newspaper at the time. Nobody would believe that they were seeing an actual airship, even though a certain E.J. Pennington said it belonged to him.

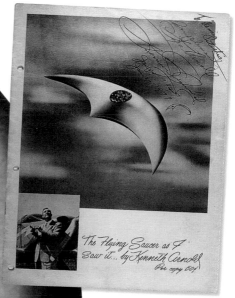

The Flying Saucer as I Saw it... by Kenneth Arnold

TUNGUSKA DISASTER

In 1908, an explosion in Siberia, Russia, flattened trees for miles around. No impact crater or meteor fragments were found, and modern theories of the cause include a comet or a small black hole. Local people, however, described an elliptical fireball that rose up from the ground. They subsequently experienced an illness resembling radiation sickness. UFOlogists suggest the phenomenon was an exploding spaceship.

UFOLOGY IS BORN

Perhaps the most influential sighting of all was made by Kenneth Arnold in the United States. In June 1947, Arnold saw nine V-shaped UFOs. He told a newspaper reporter that they moved at speeds of over 1,600 km/h (1,000 mph), 'like a saucer would if you skipped it across the water'. The newspaper's subsequent report of 'Flying Saucers' captured the public's imagination. *Fate Magazine* was published a year later, the first of many UFO publications.

FOO FIGHTERS

During the Second World War, many British and American pilots reported seeing small shining discs (which they called 'foo fighters') following their planes and causing the engines to short out. One UFOlogist thought these discs were remotely-controlled alien probes. This World War II photograph shows these mysterious discs in the sky.

THE ROSWELL INCIDENT

This artist's reconstruction of the Roswell incident shows a UFO being struck by lightning in the storm of 4 July 1947.

 FOOD FOR THOUGHT

The US government's denial of the presence of an alien spaceship may have a more common-sense explanation. They may have been trying to keep secret the presence of a Japanese 'balloon bomb' left over from World War II, or a top-secret US 'spy-balloon' designed to monitor Russian nuclear capabilities. In 1947, the US Air Force bomber group at Roswell was the world's only nuclear-weaponed strike force, and it is almost certain that the subsequent government secrecy was motivated by fear of espionage.

THE TRUTH IS OUT THERE

On 8 July, local engineer Grady Barnett added to the Roswell mystery when he and a team of archaeologists claimed to have found a crashed disc-shaped UFO and the bodies of four aliens – small, grey humanoids with large heads. The US Air Force quickly removed these, leaving nothing to be seen. Even an investigation by the US Senate in 1994 failed to convince UFO enthusiasts that their government does *not* still have the wreckage of a UFO and the corpses of aliens. The idea of a secret, crashed UFO – and of what we might learn by 'back-engineering' such a machine – is so attractive that it is impossible to eradicate such beliefs.

THE MOST FAMOUS UFO

Roswell Daily Record

RAAF Captures Flying Saucer On Ranch in Roswell Region

Claims Army Is Slacking Courts Martial

House Passes Tax Slash by Large Margin

No Details of Flying Disk Are Revealed

Some of Soviet Satellites May Attend Paris Meeting

Ex-King Carol Weds Mme. Lupescu

On 4 July 1947, there was a lightning storm over the town of Roswell in New Mexico. Sitting in his farmhouse, rancher William 'Mac' Brazel thought he heard an explosion above the sound of the storm. Next day, riding out to check his sheep, Brazel discovered some wreckage 'like nothing made on Earth'. It crumpled like foil but slowly straightened itself out again and was impervious to blows from a sledgehammer. Brazel reported it to the local air base, only to be arrested and held in custody until the wreckage had been retrieved. This was the prelude to one of the best-known and most durable UFO stories.

CAPTURED!

Since the Arnold 'flying saucer' story of June 1947, the US Air Force had recorded almost a thousand UFO sightings from all over the USA, including reports of downed spacecraft. On 8 July 1947, the commander at the Roswell Air Force base told the press that a flying disc had been recovered from a local site. Immediately, according to the *Roswell Daily Record*, the Roswell wreckage became a crashed UFO from which four aliens had been retrieved.

ALIEN AUTOPSY

In 1996, businessman Ray Santilli released film, on authenticated 1947 filmstock, of autopsies being done on the aliens retrieved from the Roswell crash. The film was like a B-class horror movie and the aliens looked nothing like those supposedly found in the Roswell crash. There was even a modern phone clearly visible in the background. Yet UFO enthusiasts were convinced by the 'evidence' of this film. This picture, from the Roswell International UFO Museum, shows a replica of the alien body from the filmed 'autopsy'.

BALLOON WRECKAGE

On the afternoon of 8 July, the US Air Force held two press conferences. A polite, fresh-faced, and very plausible young Warrant Officer showed foil debris from a weather balloon which he said was the cause of the confusion. When asked if it was the remains of a flying saucer, the young man giggled. Was the government trying to cover something up? That same month, there were a number of US Air Force cargo flights from Roswell to the top-secret Wright-Patterson Air Force base in Ohio. What they were carrying has never been satisfactorily explained.

CLOSE ENCOUNTERS

CLOSE ENCOUNTER CATEGORIES

CE1: *sighting only.*
CE2: *some physical evidence has been left (e.g. crop circles).*
CE3: *aliens have been seen.*
CE4: *alien abduction.*
CE5: *humans and aliens have met and interacted.*

 FOOD FOR THOUGHT

After four years, the Hessdalen investigators concluded that the lights were probably a natural phenomenon. There is so much about our world that we do not understand, it is highly likely that UFO incidents are, in fact, natural but rare phenomena which we cannot yet explain. Only when we understand everything about our own world will we be able to say that inexplicable events may have been caused by aliens.

CLOSE ENCOUNTERS

During the 1950s and 1960s, there were thousands of UFO sightings but it was not until 1972 that a way of analysing and categorizing them was developed by J. Allen Hynek, a respected UFOlogist. In his book *The UFO Experience*, Dr Hynek was the first UFOlogist to divide the different kinds of UFO event into types of close encounters. Ever since then, UFOlogists have classified UFO events according to his categories, from close encounters of the first kind, to close encounters of the fifth kind. Many UFOlogists also give reports of encounters a strangeness rating according to how typical of such events they are.

HESSDALEN LIGHTS

As well as photographing the lights, the researchers used radar, seismographs, infrared viewers, spectrum analysers and Geiger counters, to track and record evidence of their presence.

A CE2: PROJECT HESSDALEN, NORWAY

During 1981-85, Norwegian scientists studied lights that appeared over Hessdalen. The lights moved and seemed to respond to the actions of the observers.

CLOSE ENCOUNTERS OF THE THIRD KIND

Steven Spielberg's 1977 film was based on UFOlogist J. Allen Hynek's book, *The UFO Experience* (1972). In the story, a series of UFO encounters gradually build up to a friendly meeting between aliens and humans (a CE5). It has been suggested that the US government asked Steven Spielberg to make the film to calm public fears about UFOs.

A CE1: THE LUBBOCK LIGHTS, USA

In 1951, the people of Lubbock, Texas, reported a V-shaped formation of lights passing overhead at night. The lights were said to be travelling at about 650 km/h (400 mph). A nearby radar station also recorded an 'unknown' object. Official explanations of the phenomenon include a flight of geese illuminated by street lights, and an experimental jet bomber being tested in the area.

CATTLE MUTILATIONS, CROP CIRCLES & OTHER CE2S

CROP CIRCLES

In the 1980s, crop circles began to appear all over the world, especially in Britain and, as this example shows, in Japan. UFOlogists suggested they were made by landing spacecraft. Given celebrity status by the newspapers, the circles received a great deal of publicity.

A close encounter of the second kind is when a UFO leaves some physical evidence of its presence. In one famous example, a French farmer from Trans-en-Provence reported in 1981 that an object had landed in his garden. Government investigators found the soil had been heated to 600°C (1,112°F). One scientist suggested the effects had been produced by a strong electro-magnetic field. The story is similar to that of another farmer, M. Masse, who in 1965 claimed that a spaceship had landed in his lavender-field in Valensole – about 48 km (30 miles) from Trans-en-Provence.

A CE2 OF A DIFFERENT KIND

Stephen Michalak, an amateur geologist, claims to have seen a spaceship near Winnipeg, Canada, in 1967. Apparently, when the craft flew away the heat was so intense that his clothes were set on fire. Later, the pattern of a grille appeared burned on to Michalak's chest. Some sceptics claimed that Michalak had burned himself but scientists found evidence of radioactivity and extreme heat at the landing site.

CROP ART

One Australian suggested crop circles were caused by courting coots. A British expert blamed stampeding hedgehogs. But when a meteorologist said they were caused by stationary tornadoes, elaborate crop patterns started to appear which could not possibly have been made by the weather. This beautiful example appeared in Wiltshire, England. In 1991, two retired artists showed how they had faked many crop patterns in Britain. Strangely, many hoaxers have reported seeing UFOs while they were working on the crop patterns.

 FOOD FOR THOUGHT

Why would aliens fly 2,000 light-years to fiddle about in fields, and why would such technologically sophisticated beings need thousands of animal organs for their studies? These stories are so unbelievable that no one should ever think they are the work of alien visitors. The real danger is that, swamped by the thousands of hoaxers and cranks, our scientists may miss the one witness who has had a genuine CE2!

HOW DID SNIPPY DIE?

In 1967, a horse called *Snippy* (or *Lady* in some accounts) was found dead on a ranch in Colorado. Her head had been skinned with a straight cut and her internal organs had been removed. There was no blood on the ground, and there were circular exhaust-marks all around the body. Similar cases have been reported from all over the world, notably a large number of horse mutilations in England in the 1980s.

CATTLE MUTILATION

There have been hundreds of reports of mutilations of cattle, such as this example from New Mexico, USA. Some people suggest they are the work of Satanists, but investigations of individual animals have shown that the blood in the flesh on either side of the cuts has been cooked at a temperature of about 150°C (302°F), yet the cells around the incisions remained undamaged. Today, we know of no instruments capable of doing this.

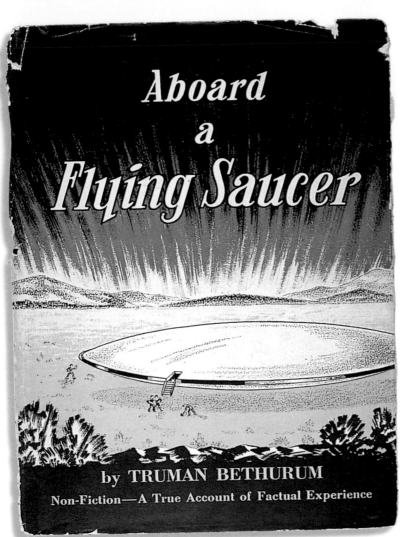

Aboard a Flying Saucer

by TRUMAN BETHURUM

Non-Fiction—A True Account of Factual Experience

TRUMAN BETHURUM
CONTACTEE, 1954

Bethurum was a road-layer who in 1954 claimed to have met aliens in the California desert near Las Vegas. His visitors had olive green skin and dark hair. They came from Clarion, a planet obscured from the Earth by the Moon. Clarion, Bethurum was told, had no disease, crime, nor politicians.

ABOARD A
FLYING SAUCER

Bethurum claimed he had actually been taken aboard the alien spaceship where he met the craft's captain, a beautiful alien called Aura Rhanes who spoke in rhyme. Bethurum met her romantically a number of times, much to the annoyance of his wife! Bethurum wrote a successful book about his experiences.

FOOD FOR THOUGHT

All this evidence, like all UFO evidence, is merely anecdotal. It confirms UFOlogy as no more than a pseudo-science, based on unsubstantiated stories and hearsay. The stories are obviously ridiculous. Today, our interest in them is not whether they are true but why so many people in the 1950s were so easily taken in by these deceptions, and what has changed in our society to make us less likely to believe such stories.

AN ALIEN IN NEW JERSEY, 1957

Born in 1922, Howard Menger says he first saw 'space-people' as a child and also had many close encounters while in the army. In his book *From Outer Space to You* (1959), he wrote about meeting Venusians, some over 500 years old. They included a number of beautiful women in transparent ski-suits – although the spacewoman in this photograph seems to be wearing a more conventional spacesuit. Menger claims to have helped the Venusians fit into Earthly society, cutting the men's long hair and offering the women bras! Menger said his second wife Marla was from Venus. In the 1960s, Menger claimed the Central Intelligence Agency (CIA) had asked him to make up the encounters so that they could test public reaction to UFO stories. He also claims men in black (see page 104) tried to prevent him talking about his sightings.

100

TAKE ME TO YOUR LEADER!

In a close encounter of the fifth kind there is interaction between aliens and humans. The great age of the contactee was the 1950s, when many books were published on the subject and meetings with space beings were described by a number of speakers at public lectures. Nowadays, UFOlogists are embarrassed by these stories which tend to discredit genuine UFO research.

JOE SIMONTON, USA

Many other people claimed to have met space visitors. One strange case was that of 60-year-old chicken farmer Joe Simonton of Wisconsin. In 1961, he was visited by small, dark-skinned spacemen wearing black suits and knitted balaclavas! The aliens asked him for a jug of water, and in return gave him some pancakes. Simonton ate one of the pancakes, which tasted like cardboard, and sent the others for analysis. They were made out of ordinary flour but with no salt. Local people said Simonton was a quiet, ordinary man who did not make up amazing stories.

FLYING SAUCERS HAVE LANDED

George Adamski was a burger-bar waiter who later gave himself the title of 'Professor'. He had written a novel about meeting a man from Venus but hadn't found a publisher. When he re-modelled his story as fact, his book *Flying Saucers Have Landed* (1953) became a bestseller.

GEORGE ADAMSKI CONTACTEE, 1953

In 1953, after seeing a UFO in the California desert, Adamski went to investigate. He met a handsome, sun-tanned young Venusian with long, sandy-coloured hair who told him – using hand signs and telepathy – that Venus was Earth's sister planet. The Venusians had come to warn humanity that nuclear radiation could ruin the Earth. Adamski later claimed to have been taken by his Venusian friends to Mars, Saturn and Jupiter.

IS ANYBODY OUT THERE?

The universe is infinite. Even if life on Earth was created by chance, the universe is so big that somewhere in the vast expanse of space the circumstances that led to life on Earth could also have occurred elsewhere. Surely infinite space cannot be devoid of other life forms? Well, so argue science fiction buffs and many UFOlogists. Out there, they say (as any *Star Trek* fan knows), there are hundreds of different races of every possible shape, size and colour. Or are there?

MARS FACE

The Viking expedition to Mars in 1976 photographed a rock formation, 3 km (2 miles) long, that looked like a face. Nearby was a collection of pyramid-shaped rocks. UFOlogists claimed it was an ancient Egyptian-like civilization on the shores of a Martian sea. But in 1998, when Mars Global Surveyor re-photographed the area from a different angle, the 'Mars Face' looked like a meteor-battered mountain – exactly what it had always been.

BEYOND OUR DREAMS

Since the nearest star to Earth is 38,000,000,000,000 km (24,000,000,000,000 miles) away, SETI thinks it is 'unlikely' aliens have visited our planet. It prefers to see UFOs as 'paranormal' phenomena. Even so, UFOlogists still find it hard to believe that, in the infinite vastness of space, there is not life out there somewhere.

SETI

The Search for Extra-terrestrial Intelligence (SETI) began on 8 April 1960. SETI radio telescopes at the huge Aricebo Observatory in Puerto Rico search for radio signals from the stars. On the first day, a regular 'whoop, whoop' was detected from a star named Epsilon Eridani. Since then, nothing.

LIFE ON MARS

In Antarctica in 1984, a meteorite was discovered that matched the Martian rock studied by the 1976 Mars Viking expedition. Scientists found organic molecules and tiny possible fossils. The excitement is not that life exists on Mars, but that life can develop on other planets.

EXTRASOLAR PLANETS

This is an artist's impression, but astronomers really have discovered planets in outer space. They use the displacements of a star's spectrum (the 'doppler shift') to detect 'wobbles' in its spinning. These betray the existence of another body in orbit around it. In October 1997, astronomers at a Swiss observatory discovered a planet circling the star 51 Pegasi. It is half the size of Jupiter, orbits just 7 million km (4,350,000 miles) from its star in a 'year' of only four days, and has a surface temperature of perhaps 1,300°C (2,372°F).

In November 1961, the American radio astronomer Frank Drake (who later became president of the SETI Institute) gave the lecture which changed our thinking about 'Is there life in space?'. The answer, he said, is a mathematical equation:

$$N = R^* \times f_p \times n_e \times f_l \times f_i \times f_c \times L$$

He explained that the number (N) of 'space' civilizations is equal to the number of Earth-type stars in the Milky Way (R*), times the fraction of stars with planets (fp), times the number of those planets capable of supporting life (ne), times the fraction of planets on which life does, by chance, occur (fl), and evolves intelligence (fi), and develops an advanced scientific civilization like ours (fc), times the number of years that the civilization survives (L). The problem with this equation is that we don't know the value of any of the factors in it. However, we can make some reasonable assumptions so that you can do the equation yourself.

1. In the Milky Way there are about 25 billion stars roughly similar to our Sun (= R*).

2. Guess that one in five have planets (so R* x fp = 25 billion x $\frac{1}{5}$).

3. Guess that each of those stars has 2 planets like Earth (ne = 2), that life evolves on one in a hundred (fl = $\frac{1}{100}$), intelligent life on a tenth of those (fi = $\frac{1}{10}$), and scientific system comparable to ours on a tenth of those (fc = $\frac{1}{10}$).

4. Guess that each of those civilizations lasts 1,000 years, in a universe which has existed at least 10,000 million years, so L = a millionth (i.e., divide by a million).

Work it out. How many Earth-like scientific civilizations are there in the Milky Way?

AREA 51, USA

According to the US government, Area 51 in Nevada does *not* exist – the area is blank on the map. In fact, it is a *secret* US air base that may be used for testing prototype military aircraft, such as unmanned aerial vehicles (above right), or for dumping waste from nuclear weapons. UFO-watchers regularly see craft performing aerial manoeuvres there at night. They believe Area 51 is where the US government has stored the Roswell UFO (see pages 94-5).

A SECRET TECHNOLOGY

According to Bob Lazar, the US Government has recovered some crashed UFOs and is 'back-engineering' their technology to see how they work.

MEN IN BLACK (MIB)

UFO witnesses have sometimes been followed by 'men in black' who look like agents of the Federal Bureau of Investigation (FBI). Some UFO-believers claim the MIB are aliens trying to suppress the truth. Or perhaps they *are* FBI agents. This MIB is from the Hollywood film of the same name.

AREA 51: CONSPIRACY

'Don't be fooled!' say **UFO** enthusiasts. 'Aliens do exist. The government knows about them and has worked with them for many years. But there is a cover-up to stop you getting to know.' To be a UFO-believer, it is almost necessary to be a conspiracy-believer. Conspiracy theories are immune to contradiction because they are beyond proof or disproof. No matter what a government does or says, the conspiracy-believer shouts, 'trick'. Even when a claim is proved to be ridiculous or a hoax, conspiracy-believers simply assert that they have been misinformed by the government in order to discredit them.

BOB LAZAR

According to Bob Lazar, who claims he once worked at Area 51, the US government has nine UFOs stored there. Although there is no evidence that Lazar ever worked at Area 51, nor of his gaining an engineering degree from the university he claims to have attended, his testimony is often taken as proof that there is a conspiracy to cover up the truth!

MAJESTIC 12

In 1984, a TV company was sent some documents on photographic film. They seemed to prove that a group of experts called the Majestic 12 had been set up in 1947 to study the Roswell UFO. The fact that the documents had been typed on a typewriter not invented until 1963 was ignored, and conspiracy-believers still think they prove the US government has a UFO. They say if the documents were faked, they were faked by the government in a conscious attempt at disinformation!

**TOP SECRET
EYES ONLY**

THE WHITE HOUSE
WASHINGTON

September 24, 1947.

MEMORANDUM FOR THE SECRETARY OF DEFENSE

Dear Secretary Forrestal,

As per our recent conversation on this matter, you are hereby authorized to proceed with all due speed and caution upon your undertaking. Hereafter this matter shall be referred to only as Operation Majestic Twelve.

It continues to be my feeling that any future considerations relative to the ultimate disposition of this matter should rest solely with the Office of the President following appropriate discussions with yourself, Dr. Bush and the Director of Central Intelligence.

**TOP SECRET
EYES ONLY**

FOOD FOR THOUGHT

The American psychologist Elaine Showalter believes conspiracy theories are deeply damaging to society because they poison our faith in our institutions. We used to believe we could always ask a policeman for help. Now, we feel that no matter who we elect no government official or department can be trusted. Conspiracy-believers have made the world a frightening and lonely place.

WHAT SHOULD I DO IF I MEET AN ALIEN?

Many **UFO** enthusiasts believe that aliens are among us. One crank on the Internet claims to have located 136 alien bases on Earth, with 14,619 aliens and a 'robot army' of about 5,000 humans implanted with mind-controlling chips. Science fiction has imagined ever more sinister aliens, in a variety of different forms. The sequence of Alien films depict beings impervious to human technology. They have acid for blood, no feelings or morality, and use humans as host incubators. The prospect of humankind ever being visited by such entities is terrifying. So, what kind of alien are you likely to encounter out on the moors on a dark and stormy night?

NORDICS

This actor from the TV series *Alien Nation* illustrates another type – tall, Scandinavian-looking aliens from Sirius, Pleiades, or Venus. They are spiritual, gentle, and love humans, and claim their ancestors were the first human beings – but watch out! Some of them have been captured by the Greys and fitted with implants to enslave them.

 FOOD FOR THOUGHT

If you meet an alien, RUN! Modern UFO writers don't claim all aliens are dangerous but there is enough evidence to convince you not to take the risk.
SETI have sent radio messages into space. The 1977 Voyager Space probe carried the message 'Greetings. We step out into the universe seeking only peaceful contact.' They may as well have said, 'Please come and eat us!' A common feature of abduction reports is that the aliens take small meaningless things from humans. In one story, aliens stole a bunch of flowers from a woman. In another, they took fishing flies and banknotes. So, if you can't run from the aliens, be sure to have some attractive trinket on you. It might distract them while you get away!

CHUPACABRAS (GOAT-EATERS)

This group of aliens are said to live in the caves of Puerto Rico. Measuring a little over I metre (3 ft) tall, they have huge red eyes, fangs, long claws, and vampire-wings. They come out at night to mutilate, kill and eat livestock. Some UFOlogists think they are the crew of a crashed spaceship, but they may be creatures that escaped into the jungle when a hurricane destroyed a secret government research installation.

MIDGET MARTIANS

Like these midgets from the film *The Man in the Moon*, aliens may be from a highly developed civilization, be loving and lovable, and will usher in a world of health and happiness!

THE GREYS

Greys are the aliens typical of most abduction stories, about 1.5 metres (4½ ft) tall with large heads and wrap-around eyes. They come from Andromeda or Zeta Reticuli. Their military, totalitarian society aims to conquer Earth and make us their slaves. They have no feelings, and conduct their medical and genetic experiments without anaesthetic.

THE WORLD'S MYSTERIES EXPLORED

FATE

JANUARY 1978 75¢

DEATH BY
HELL'S FIRE

CLOSE ENCOUNTERS OF THE THIRD KIND

REPORT A UFO
AT YOUR OWN RISK

. . .Plus Many Other
Intriguing Features

GREEN-SKINNED MONSTERS

Reports say that UFOs can 'turn off' human technology and shoot down military planes. They have paralysing beams and can abduct whole regiments of men. They do nasty experiments on people. If they exist, these beings are far more advanced than us, and they are dangerous!

FOOD FOR THOUGHT

One in six people need psychiatric help at some time in their adult life. 'Abduction' experiences are probably a form of mental delusion. The Hills and the Walton cases (see pages 110-111) both illustrate the power of television to influence our subconscious minds. Even under hypnosis it is possible to tell lies, and there is considerable evidence that hypnotists can 'suggest' UFO ideas to an abductee. Indeed, experiments have been done in which subjects were able to invent realistic 'imaginary abductions' under hypnosis. People have been observed having an abduction experience. In one case in Australia, two people watched as someone (who never left their sight) apparently 'met' aliens and 'went into' a spaceship. It was clearly a real event inside the head of the 'abductee' but all the two witnesses saw was the abductee's physical responses to what he seemed to be experiencing. Most abduction 'memories' are similar. They involve tunnels, lights, being covered in liquid, finding it hard to breathe, pain in the navel, being medically examined, etc. Women abductees remember having eggs taken from their ovaries, or even being implanted with alien foetuses. In these details, most 'abductions' seem more like a flashback to the experience of being born rather than of an alien encounter.

ABDUCTION CASEBOOK

In the **USA**, a recent survey suggested one in **20** people believe they have been abducted. **One UFO**logist claims we have all been abducted at one time or another! Many victims only realize they have been abducted after their memories are drawn out by regression therapy (by which a hypnotist takes them back to re-live events in their past). A phenomenon which involves so many people is certainly worth investigation.

ALL OF THE FOLLOWING SYMPTOMS HAVE BEEN CONSIDERED EVIDENCE OF AN ABDUCTION

- 'Lost' time, which cannot be accounted for.
- Scars, bruises or burns with no memory of what caused them.
- Nightmares, especially about aliens, flying, or being eaten by animals with large eyes (such as owls).
- Insomnia, especially when caused by fear of going sleep.
- Medical problems, such as vomiting, headaches, tiredness, or rashes.
- Depression.
- A UFO sighting; experience of déjà vu; or a feeling of having 'second sight', the ability to foresee the future or see events happening elsewhere.
- An image repeatedly comes to mind (perhaps put in the brain to block memory).
- Unaccountable black marks on an X-ray.

IMPLANTS

Some UFOlogists believe aliens implant tracking devices in the people they abduct so that they can locate them later. This implant was found in the roof of an abductee's mouth. Above, 17-year-old abductee James Basel with his alleged alien implant.

CASE STUDY 1: ANTONIO VILLAS BOAS, BRAZIL

Name/Occupation: Antonio Villas Boas. Farmer.

Date: Approx. 16 October 1957.

Location: Francisco de Sales, Brazil.

Case Description: The day after seeing a UFO, Villas Boas was alone on his tractor, ploughing a field. Dragged on board an egg-shaped craft by three humanoids, he was stripped, covered in a clear liquid, and had a blood sample taken from his chin.

Investigator's Notes: Villas Boas tried to fight off his abductors. Doctors found marks and scars all over his body. He suffered sickness and sleepiness which resembled radiation poisoning. Villas Boas remembered his experience without regression therapy and never changed his story. Boas remembered seeing some writing over the door of the UFO craft.

An artist's impression of one of Antonio's abductors and the alien craft that landed in his field.

CASE STUDY 2: BETTY AND BARNEY HILL, USA

Name/Occupation: Betty (retired social worker) and Barney Hill.

Date: 19 September 1961.

Location: New Hampshire, USA.

Case Description: On their way home one evening, Betty and Barney were frightened by a UFO. They later found marks on their bodies and realized they had 'lost' two hours. Nightmares and depression followed. Under regression hypnosis they remembered being abducted by creatures with 'wrap-around' eyes. A needle had been inserted into Betty's navel.

Betty remembered a 'star map' the aliens had shown her and drew a copy of it. From this, UFOlogists deduced the aliens came from Zeta Reticuli, about 30 light years from Earth.

Investigator's Notes: Although the Hills are often described as an 'ordinary couple', Betty has had many psychic experiences. At one time, she claimed UFOs followed her everywhere. Her psychiatrist believed she was suffering delusions after a frightening experience and that her husband had adopted her anxieties into his own memory. Their abduction happened shortly after a sci-fi programme on TV had depicted aliens with 'wrap-around' eyes.

An artist's impression of Betty and Barney during their encounter with a UFO.

CASE STUDY 3: TRAVIS WALTON, USA

Name/Occupation: Travis Walton. Forester.

Date: 5 November 1975.

Location: Arizona, USA.

Case Description: One night in November 1975, the seven men of a logging team saw a UFO. When Walton went to investigate he was paralysed by a beam of light from the craft. His friends fled, leaving him for dead. Five days later, Walton turned up in a nearby town. Under regression hypnosis he remembered a typical abduction. He was examined by three tall aliens with large eyes, and was shown a hangar full of UFOs.

Investigator's Notes: The Hills's abduction story had appeared on TV only a month before this incident. The team were behind on their logging contract and wanted an excuse. Travis Walton was known as a practical joker. But, 25 years later, not one of the seven-man team had changed his story.

Travis Walton wrote a book. His experience was made into a film, Fire in the Sky, in which some of the facts were changed. Nonetheless, the team made a lot of money from their story.

CASE STUDY 4: LINDA NAPOLITANO, USA

Name/Occupation: Linda Napolitano. Housewife.

Date: 30 November 1989.

Location: New York, USA.

Case Description: In 1989, Linda Napolitano was having hypnosis therapy because she believed she had been abducted a number of times. During her treatment, she revealed she had been abducted again. Under hypnosis, Linda remembered being taken out through the walls of her 12th-storey apartment into a spaceship high above the streets of Manhattan. She was medically examined, then returned to her bed.

Investigator's Notes: In 1991, this amazing story was given credence when two Manhattan police officers, who later claimed to be secret service men, reported that they had seen a woman floating in the sky and being taken into a UFO. Later, another witness also claimed to have seen the event.

An artist's impression of Linda Napolitana's abduction from her Manhattan apartment.

FAKES

ROSWELL REVISITED

This effect, taken at Roswell, USA, was achieved by photographing a UFO-like object thrown towards the setting sun.

UFOlogy is a tempting field for con-men who want to make money, and publicity-seekers who want to be famous. Some of the best work to expose fakes is done by responsible UFOlogists who know that fraudulent claims only add to public and government scepticism. The pictures on these pages show how some of the people can be fooled some of the time.

VENUSIAN SCOUT CRAFT

Effects (FX) technology has improved so much that some past fakes now look ridiculous. This photograph of a 'scout craft' taken by George Adamski (see page 101) looks no more sophisticated than a metal lampshade and some light bulbs. What Venusian would be brave enough to set off across the solar system in one of these?

🐦 FOOD FOR THOUGHT

UFO photographers can't win, can they? Blurred blobs are rejected as too indistinct to show anything; brilliant images are dismissed as too good to be true. Nevertheless, after a century of UFO interest in the camera age, there is not one, unquestioned, clear photograph of a UFO.

STRANGE CLOUDS, HAWAII

Photographed near Hawaii, this UFO is, in fact, a lenticular cloud formation, lit by the rays of the setting sun.

FAKE UFO?

Modern FX technology makes it more difficult to distinguish the fake from the real. What is suspicious about this UFO shot?

ALPINE FAKE, ITALY

This UFO in the Bernina Mountains is probably a table-top model, photographed close up. The spacesuited alien is almost certainly a toy soldier. It was exposed as a fake by the Italian Ufologico Nationale.

HOW TO DETECT A FAKE PHOTOGRAPH

- *Lack of adequate perspective reference that would indicate the size and position of an object, suggests that the UFO is a model that has been hung up or thrown.*
- *Variations in the grain of a photo indicate an image has been 'pasted' into it.*
- *Irregularities in the angles of light (and shadows) between the object and the background are evidence of separate images pasted together.*
- *Differences in colour, clarity, or brightness between the UFO and the rest of the photo are often a sign that the UFO has been painted or stuck on to a pane of glass in front of the camera.*
- *Bright luminous blobs or streaks may be blemishes on the film negative, or lens flare and reflection. These account for many UFO pictures caught by accident.*
- *Such things as tree branches or telephone lines above a UFO indicate that an object might have been hung up close to the camera.*
- *Photographs conveniently blurred, fuzzy, or indistinct, suggest a model which the photographer has tried to disguise.*

SHARING THE MESSAGE

A constant theme of abduction stories is the 'message to save mankind', usually a warning about the dangers of nuclear weapons or environmental pollution. 1950s contactee Howard Menger claimed that space people gave him a model of the perpetual motion engine that powered their spacecraft, as well as some potatoes from the Moon. But why travel across the universe to tell us something we know already? And, having travelled trillions of miles, why give the message to Joe Nobody of Backwoodsville? Why not tell the president of a powerful nation?

GLOBAL CONQUEST

This is a favourite theme of sci-fi films such as *Independence Day*. Some UFO enthusiasts genuinely believe there are aliens on Earth who are preparing for invasion and conquest by spreading new diseases and interfering with our weather. But if global conquest is their aim, why are aliens with the technology to cross the universe taking decades, millennia even, to take over the Earth?

DESPERATE FOR DNA

Some UFO-watchers think aliens are sterile or genetically mutated, and are seeking to restore their health by 'splicing' our DNA with their own. But why would aliens with the science to cross the universe need so many hundreds of abductees for their experiments?

WHY ARE THEY HERE?

The main flaw in all accounts of alien visitors is how they got here. One respected UFOlogist thinks there are alien civilizations in the galaxy but the nearest is 2,000 light years away. Travelling at the speed of light sounds feasible in science fiction. In reality, the technology to 'fold space' or to reconstitute at its destination a being who has been 'transported', seems impossible.

For travellers at the speed of light, time comes to a standstill. In the time it takes to think, 'I must stop now,' they would travel an infinite distance in (for the rest of us) an infinite amount of time. They would end up beyond the universe at a time when everyone and everything was long since dead. And, given the difficulty of getting here, why should aliens want to visit the Earth? What have we got that they could possibly want? Until we meet one who can tell us, theories abound! Some of them are shown on these pages.

SCIENTIFIC EXPERIMENTS

Some UFO enthusiasts believe the human race is a huge genetic experiment. Some think that because aliens have no emotions they want to study concepts such as love, fear, and pain. This cover picture from a 1935 magazine shows that these ideas have a long history.

INTER-GALACTIC TOURISM

The film, *Morons from Outer Space*, in which a group of extra-terrestrial tourists (literally) bump into the Earth, suggests another possible reason. Perhaps the Earth is a galactic wildlife sanctuary run by aliens. Their rangers come to check that the human animals are healthy. Visitors are meant to stay out of sight but sometimes they become over-inquisitive or accidentally knock off the invisibility button. And, of course, there is limited hunting!

 FOOD FOR THOUGHT

The problem with all of these theories is the discrepancy between the sophistication needed to cross the universe to get to Earth, and the lack of progress the aliens make when they get here. Whether they come as scientific human-watchers trying to stay hidden, conquerors trying to overwhelm us, or do-gooders with a message to impart, after 50 years they have all proved singularly incompetent in achieving their aim!

TIME-SLIP

Occasionally, radio-waves seem to 'wobble' and listeners find their programme interrupted briefly by a completely different channel. We imagine time as a knife-edge rushing along with a void before it and obliteration behind it. But if time were like a radio signal that can sometimes wobble, UFOs might be a random glimpse of the future. Time-slip would also explain things like sightings of the Loch Ness monster, of ghosts and the 'walking dead', and of disorienting experiences such as *déjà vu*, in which we have a sense of something having happened before.

THEORIES

Some UFOlogists think the popular definition of an alien as an extraterrestrial (ET) is misleading. Today, most UFOlogists accept it is unlikely that Earth is being visited from other galaxies. Instead, they prefer to define alien as 'something outside normal human experience'. Perhaps, some say, aliens are a spiritual manifestation. A 1950s contactee, Richard Miller, claimed an alien from Alpha Centauri told him UFOs were angels. Other people believe UFOs are demons. The founder of the Aetherius Society, George King (a London taxi driver recruited by aliens in 1954 to help save the world from an intelligent meteor) claimed Jesus Christ was an alien from Venus. Other UFOlogists assert that UFO experiences are a real phenomenon but seek explanations which do not involve little green men in spaceships.

THE 'OZ' FACTOR

Known as the Oz factor, a still and eerie quiet is often reported to occur just prior to an alien encounter. UFOlogist Jenny Randles draws attention to the similarity between UFO events and paranormal phenomena such as extra-sensory perception (ESP), out-of-body, and near-death experiences. She accepts the possibility of other beings in the universe but wonders if they are trying to get in touch on a psychic level.

ANOTHER DIMENSION

UFO experiences may be the result of our three-dimensional world co-existing with other worlds that have more or fewer dimensions. A creature living in a two-dimensional world would have no height, only length and breadth (like a sheet of paper). Such a creature would not be able to see up or down, as 'up' and 'down' would not exist in its two-dimensional world. It would only be aware of a very thin slice of the universe.

Now imagine if a ball were to pass through this creature's world. Until the ball broke through, the creature would be unaware of it altogether. Then it would see a mysterious circular shape appearing, growing in diameter, then getting smaller again and finally disappearing as the ball finished passing through.

If Earth shares space with and occasionally overlaps other-dimensional worlds, then glimpses of these would be just as fleeting and puzzling for us.

WAKING DREAMS

These psychological experiences can be so vivid that in the dreamer's memory it may not be clear what was dream and what was reality. Many waking dreams are disorienting, terrifying events. Later, to come to terms with the trauma the brain might assign to it a symbolic but nevertheless concrete and explicable reality. In the past, people blamed ghosts or demons for their hallucinations but, today, because sci-fi images and sophisticated technology are familiar to us, our brain is likely to attribute such experiences to aliens.

MODERN GHOSTS

In these enlightened times of scientific reason and logic, we might assume that most supernatural matters would by now have been sufficiently well investigated for us to take a rational view about them. One certainly might expect the belief in ghosts to be on the wane, but it is not. There has probably never been more interest, and ghostly manifestations continue to be reported. While many of these may be hoaxes, there is a growing weight of evidence to suggest that ghosts do exist.

CAUGHT IN THE BEAM

In 1965, at Bluebell Hill, in Kent, three young girls were tragically killed in a motoring accident. The ghost of one of them still wanders the stretch of road, and the local police station often receives reports from drivers who think they have knocked someone down. When they get out to investigate they find no one there. Sometimes the girl hitches a lift and gets into a passing car but then mysteriously disappears. A similar story persists in Norway, where a sign has been erected on the roadside warning motorists not to pick up the ghostly hitchhiker.

MESSAGES FROM THE GRAVE

The answering machine of a Jules and Maggie Harsch-Fischbach from Luxembourg is allegedly haunted and regularly receives complex messages from dead scientists. Research into the life force that seems to occupy some inanimate objects suggests that they could be haunted by a previous owner who has left a mental imprint on them, psychokinetically.

FACES OF DEATH

In 1971, in the village of Bélmez in southern Spain, a ghostly human face suddenly imprinted itself on the pink floor tiles of a kitchen. When the family tried to rub off the troubled-looking face, its eyes opened wider and its expression saddened. The owner tore up the tiles and laid a concrete floor but another more clearly-defined face appeared. Experts in the paranormal were called in to investigate, and strange moaning sounds were recorded. Later, the house was found to be above an old cemetery.

THE WHITE HOUSE

The White House in Washington DC is haunted by a number of the past presidents of the United States. Several ghosts are attributed to Abraham Lincoln, who was assassinated in 1865. His distinctive image has been seen by such notable personages as Queen Wilhelmina of the Netherlands while staying there, and by President Reagan's daughter during his incumbency. Lincoln himself believed in spiritualism and attended several seances at the White House, which may account for his powerful presence still being felt there today.

FOOD FOR THOUGHT

An often overlooked aspect of ghosts is the powerful effect that wishful thinking can have on the human mind. The power of positive thought is very real and is taken seriously by doctors and scientists. After the death of a famous and much-loved person, such as Elvis, we long for them to live again. This sense of grief may be so strong that it could enable the human mind to externalize a familiar image which we then allow ourselves to believe is the ghost of the person we love.

DOES THE KING LIVE ON?

Elvis Presley (1935-77) became one of the most idolized entertainers of his time. To many people he remains the ultimate rock-and-roll star. When he died in tragic circumstances, many of his devoted fans refused to accept it. Since 1977, he has supposedly been sighted in a variety of places worldwide, not just in America.

MODERN MONSTERS

Although we like to think we are less gullible than our ancestors, modern people find just as many things to be afraid of. But the monsters that scare us today are no longer dragons in the sea or goblins in the forests. We live in a scientific, technological age which creates its own monsters. The instinct to feel fear is part of our heritage. It may keep us awake at night or send shivers down our spine, but it also alerts us to look both ways when we cross the road, or to stay away from dangerous animals and situations. Dragons, giants and goblins may have disappeared into the story-books, but that doesn't mean there is nothing to be afraid of. In modern times, there are more monsters than ever.

MINI-MONSTERS

Just as our forebears feared the 'little people', we have something tiny of our own to worry about. Our improved scientific understanding of what causes diseases has given us something very real to fear. We now know that under a microscope we can see scarier creatures than we could ever imagine – viruses, bacteria, and other tiny disease-carrying organisms. Even the ordinary head louse above looks monstrous.

FOOD FOR THOUGHT

Science can explain the dark and the animalistic, but it can't stop people being afraid. There will always be things we do not understand. Everything we learn uncovers another mystery, another monster, another scary story. Modern monsters are not borne out of superstition or religious beliefs, but out of science and technology. We can see the tiny monsters that make us ill; we imagine the terror of machinery gone mad, a world poisoned, or a bomb to end all bombs. As long as there are stories to tell, so there will be monsters to fear.

IRRATIONAL FEARS

Today, we are better educated and more worldly-wise than our ancestors but that doesn't stop us finding plenty to feel afraid of. Intense irrational fears are called phobias of which there are many, including: claustrophobia, a fear of enclosed spaces; acrophobia, a dread of heights; agoraphobia, a fear of open spaces; arachnophobia, a fear of spiders. We know perfectly well that most spiders are harmless, yet many people are terrified of them all. Some people are even afraid of moths. So it seems monsters are still the product of our own minds.

THE ATOM

The atom is one of the tiniest building blocks of the universe, and the discovery that we could split it has unleashed one of the most devastating weapons known to man. Nuclear weapons are now *the* most terrifyingly destructive monsters of the modern world.

ALIENS

Even though almost every inch of the Earth has been mapped and millions of its creatures chronicled, some believe that there may be aliens out there somewhere – and if not already here, then on their way. Invasion and abduction by aliens are popular themes in science fiction stories. It is almost as if we have a real need for an external enemy on whom to focus our fears.

RISE OF THE ROBOTS

Computers are taking over more and more of our lives. Robots help to build cars and even perform surgical operations. But what if they go wrong? What if a computer bug makes a program work badly, or a virus destroys it. Computers fly planes, run banks, and operate hospital equipment. What if the machines decided to run things without humans? It's a silly idea, but is it any sillier than the tale of a mountain gorilla, or the idea that lightning could save somebody's life?

POLLUTION

In many ways, what we humans fear most is ourselves. As mankind uses more and more of the Earth's resources, we worry that there will be nothing left for our descendants to enjoy. The more of us there are, the more things we manufacture, and the more pollution we create. Perhaps we are the worst monsters of all.

PLACES OF POWER

LINES OF POWER

Ley lines are channels of power that supposedly run all over the Earth. Some people believe dowsers can harness these forces to help them find water or metals. It has been suggested that ley lines may have been constructed by primitive man or an ancient advanced civilization, or are simply natural features of the Earth. Large monuments or standing stones often indicate the presence of ley lines nearby. It has also been suggested that ley lines may be detectable by variations in radio waves. In England, ley lines are believed to cross Glastonbury Tor (above), a place of great religious significance.

Oespite all the research into the subject, psychic phenomena remain as enigmas. We cannot say with any certainty whether or not they genuinely exist or how they function, but, just as our ancestors were, we are fascinated by psychic power and its potential uses. Over the centuries, the mystery of psychic phenomena has inspired many attempts to harness powers of the unknown. The legacy of those attempts is scattered across the world in the form of places of power. Some are natural sites in the landscape that are considered sacred. Others were built as a centre for religious beliefs, magical practices, or primitive superstitions. These ancient places are thought to symbolize psychic forces which we do not yet understand.

MAGIC OF THE ANCIENTS

The pyramids at Giza are some of the oldest surviving man-made structures in the world. They were built before 2500 BCE by Egyptian pharaohs to entomb their mummified bodies and the valuable possessions that accompanied them into the afterlife to signify how rich and powerful they were. From the dimensions of the Great Pyramid, modern mathematicians have worked out that ancient Egyptians knew the value of pi, the number of days Earth takes to circle the Sun, and the dates of important events in the future. Recently, it has been suggested that the position of the pyramids in relation to one another is identical to the layout of stars in the constellation of Orion.

SACRED SITES OF THE ANCESTORS

Ayers Rock (Mount Uluru) in the Northern Territory of Australia is the largest single rock formation in the world and is a place of strong spiritual significance to the Aboriginal people. Many of the stories concerning Uluru are secret and are never repeated to outsiders. Around Uluru are many ancestral sites and out of respect for Aboriginal beliefs, the Australian government has restricted tourist access to them.

STANDING STONES

Stonehenge in Britain was built around 1200 BCE but we do not know for what purpose. It may have been an astronomical observatory, a Druid religious centre, or a burial ground. In 1977, the Dragon Project was established to study electrical and magnetic forces around Stonehenge and similar monuments. There are many other standing stone monuments in the world. Some of the most impressive are Carnac in Brittany, Msoura in Morocco, and at Lake Turkana in Kenya.

FOOD FOR THOUGHT

Everyone feels a sense of awe and mystery when at one of these tremendous places of power. You don't have to share the beliefs of the people who built them, or those who use them today, to be amazed by the vision, dedication, effort and genius that went into their construction. One of the most valuable things to remember about the power of the mind is that our ancestors, even if they had different beliefs to us, were just as intelligent and capable of achieving great things as we are.

WHY ARE WE SO INTERESTED?

In 1960, two French writers, Jacques Bergier and Louis Pauwels, published *The Morning of the Magicians*, a book which argued that science didn't have all the answers. Society, they said, was like a car speeding along a motorway – it was going somewhere all right, but what about the fields and villages on either side? By heading off down the science/technology road, they suggested, humankind was missing many of the important truths about life. The book revived interest in experiences that couldn't be scientifically explained. Perhaps part of the reason people are so interested in UFOs is that they are, and remain, a mystery, despite the many theories about them.

ESCAPISM

Prince Gautama Siddhartha (Buddha) lived in a palace and never saw the real world. One day, he went out and was so horrified by the suffering he saw that he left the palace for ever. Today, we see the miseries of the world on television all the time. In a sense, we enjoy 'going back into the palace' – getting away from reality and into a fantasy world.

FOOD FOR THOUGHT

Interest in UFOs and stories about alien encounters is probably here to stay. We are intrinsically fascinated by the unknown and the frightening. In a world where we are realizing that hating other groups of human beings is wrong, perhaps we need the idea of some external threat such as sinister aliens – if only to play the 'baddies' in the movies! Extraterrestrial UFOs can never be debunked, because science can prove only that something does exist, not that it doesn't.

THE MARTIANS ARE COMING!

In 1938, a radio adaptation of *The War of the Worlds*, a book by H.G. Wells, was so realistic it created panic when broadcast in America. Despite regular announcements that the play was fictional, William Dock, 76, from Grover's Mill, USA (where Martians had supposedly landed) was ready with a shotgun to ward off the imaginary invaders. People almost seemed to want the story to be true!

CLAS*Illus*

Featuring St World's Grea

No. 124 15¢

THE WAR OF THE WORLDS

By H. G. WELLS

THE RISE OF SCI-FI

Science-fiction began in the 19th century, when it seemed that science would eventually be able to do anything. Readers found it fascinating, frightening, and exciting. Today, interest in science-fiction is stronger than ever, and programmes like *Star Trek* have huge, cult followings.

THE SEARCH FOR SOMETHING BEYOND OURSELVES

The psychological need for 'something out there' that is bigger than we are is as old as humankind. Today, fewer people go to church but the need for something beyond themselves can lead to a belief in the occult or the paranormal. Interest in UFOs is perhaps part of this. One example is the Aetherius Society. Another is the *Urantia Book* which was written in the 1930s by Dr William Sadler, a psychiatrist and theologian. The *Urantia Book* teaches that the universe is full of many beings – gods, angels and mortals (among which are human beings). It is not a religion but people do attend study fellowships about it.

A SUBCONSCIOUS IMAGE

In his 1958 book, *Flying Saucers, a Modern Myth*, the great psychologist Carl Jung called UFOs a 'rumour'. He said UFOs appeal to our subconscious – even their circular shape is a powerful subconscious image – and embody our deepest hopes and fears that science and technology will either save or destroy us. He concluded that to be fascinated by UFOs is a natural and inevitable function of our psychology.

INDEX

INDEX